# Rosie

## The Story of Unfailing Love

Mary,
Diane Headen
11-03-01

Rose Marie Jones

# Rosie . . .
## The Story of Unfailing Love

ISBN 0-9669396-2-X
Library of Congress Catalog Card Number: 2001093743

Printed in the United States of America

Published by Voice Publishing
54 Albion Street
Jacksonville, Illinois 62650

D. M. Headen, editor
M. R. Jones, cover designer
J. K. Kafer, Branstiter Printing Co.

Publisher's Cataloging-in-Publication
*(Provided by Quality Books, Inc.)*

Jones, Rose Marie.
   Rosie-- : the story of unfailing love / Rose Marie
Jones ; D.M. Headen, editor ;  M.R. Jones, cover
designer. -- 1st ed.
   p. cm.
   Includes index.
   LCCN 2001093743
   ISBN 0-9669396-2-x

   1. Marriage--Religious aspects--Christianity--
Fiction.  2. Family--Religious aspects--Christianity--
Fiction.  3. Christian life--Fiction.  I. Title.

PS3560.O5268R67 2002          813'.6
                    QBI01-701078

# CONTENTS

# Prologue

Most men could confine in one volume the wisdom gained in a lifetime by their toil and prayer on this earth. Perhaps, in Heaven's library, every man's life is written as a biography, and one of our eternal pleasures will be to experience the victories and glean from the tribulations of the saints' eternal wisdom of God.

It is with this hope in mind that I dedicate *Rosie,* like one of Heaven's books dropped into earth's hands. May it whet your appetite for citizenship in the Eternal City where no darkness dwells, where your own Book of Life is being recorded.

*Rosie* is a fictional story; although, reflections of my life glimmer through the poetry.

My prayer is that *Rosie* will demonstrate divine purpose and destiny being accomplished not by human might and power but by the flow and energy of the Holy Spirit.

For my Father's glory,

Rose Marie Jones

*Chapter One*

# The Wedding

"Ladies and gentlemen, I introduce to you Mr. and Mrs. Chad Windelton!" announced Pastor Newberry to the crowd of 300 family and friends who had gathered to witness the marriage of Rose Jacquelyn Hardy and Chad Newingham Windelton. The August-first afternoon sun shone through the stained glass windows as the pipe organ echoed the pastor's declaration. With the crowd applauding, Rosie's tear-filled gaze fondly rested upon her dad and mom seated on the front pew. Rosie wanted to hug each person in the sanctuary, but especially her mother who had been her best friend through most of her teenage years. They had carefully planned the wedding together, detail by detail. Rosie had sought to please this special woman and wanted the wedding to fulfill her mom's heart's desires in every way.

Rosie's twenty-two years of life flashed before her in split second scenarios as she realized this was a holy day bridging childhood to adulthood. While growing up, she had been nurtured by a full-time, homemaking mother, Louise Hardy, whose career had been the raising of four children at her husband's side. Rosie fondly recalled a poem she had written about her mother's gift of love:

*I used to bake chocolate chip cookies*
*With my mother.*
*I remember. . .*
*I would snitch some batter,*
*And her soft, assuring eyes*
*Would sparkle in pretended disgust.*
*Oh, Mother,*
*You so loved your little mischievous bundle!*
*And when I would cry*
*Over some deceased gold fish or scraped knee,*
*You would take me in your arms and love me,*
*But not too long or too much—*
*Simply enough to patch the wound,*
*And then you would stand me up*
*Tall and straight,*
*Push my shoulders back,*
*And cause me to smile and laugh*
*Within the gaiety of the moment.*
*And I would be fine forever it seemed.*
*Mother, your love has been so giving.*
*Thank You, Lord, thank You.*

Mr. and Mrs. Chad Windelton! Rosie was breathless. Her childhood dreams of a Christian marriage were crystallizing before her eyes. Chad at age 16 first met Rosie at naive 15. They had been special friends through both high school and college. "Rosie, let's go!" Chad sweetly whispered in his new bride's ear, gently hooking her arm into his. Grasping her bouquet of talisman roses and lily of the valley, they descended the altar steps in youthful exuberance and joy.

Rosie bent to envelop her mom with a heart-piercing hug. "I love you . . . thank you!" Her dad, Frank, and mother had nurtured her with their own "marriage from Heaven" that most only dream about. This had become blatantly clear in college as Rosie became acquainted with many others' adverse home lives. Rosie's own happiness and girl-like innocence was the fruit of this perfect love between a man and woman rooted in God's love, blossoming out to church, family, and friends. She had never known a reason to entertain self-pity, had never heard a harsh word between her parents. God had placed her in a nest of committed and Christian marital love, and Rosie anticipated equally as much from her own life as Chad's wife.

The newlyweds laughed as they crammed cake into one another's mouths. "I didn't even say my vows!" Rosie playfully made fun of herself. She had contained her composure through the service until her eyes locked into Chad's. Choking up with a fountain of tears, Rosie had been prevented from speaking, so the pastor had softly whispered them for her.

"I love you," spoke Chad as he stroked her soft cheek. Rosie's three dreams of youth had now been met. Since five years of age, she had wanted to be a drum majorette, which she achieved her senior year of high school. The dream to write a book was fulfilled through her college senior-graduation project, the publication of her first book of poetry. Today, her third dream was beginning to unfold, the perpetuation of her Christian heritage with a man who deeply cherished her and vowed to pursue a life together in God.

Rosie's long, auburn hair fell softly against her

white lace veil, her blue eyes sparkling with the graciousness of a queen. She and her knight in shining armour greeted their guests as she reveled in the fulfillment of her childhood dream.

Pastor Newberry's words echoed within the walls of her mind as she repeatedly embraced her loved ones, "You have entered into a holy covenant with God and Chad . . . for better or for worse." Not in Rosie's wildest imagination could she have been able to foresee the test of that commitment which lay ahead.

*Chapter Two*

# The Honeymoon

"Chad, look at the church set against the pretty sunrise!" Rosie pointed to a Baptist church, white with towering steeple, nestled against the side of gentle, rolling hills, reminding her of one of those calendar pictures her dad's plumbing business annually issued. It was Sunday morning, and Rosie, still basking from the dreamish intimacy of their first night together, was like a little puppy dog. Her early-rising personality wagged delightfully as she requested, "Let's go to church today!" Rosie pointed through the mauve curtains toward the church yard adjacent to the hotel parking lot.

"Why are you up, woman? It's too early," the exhausted groom moaned. Rosie sheepishly pulled away from the window and sank into the chair near the table where her Bible rested from their devotions the night before. She fondly caressed its leather cover, clutching it close to her breast, and in being reminded of a teddy bear, with pen in hand, reached for a strewn wedding napkin and scratched:

> *Bible, I cling to you*
> *like a child grasping a teddy bear.*
> *In the evening your Word rocks me to sleep.*

*In the early morning*
*You await me like a best friend.*
*I thumb through your onion skin pages*
*knowing the security of a sword.*
*I cuddle with you and caress your leather back.*
*You go with me wherever I go.*
*No wonder I love you so.*
*Your companionship never ends!*

Rosie slipped the napkin in the back of her Bible as she turned her teddy bear's pages to **Psalm 119** and meditated on a favorite highlighted verse:

**"How can a young man cleanse his way?**
**By taking heed according to Your Word."**

*vs. 9*

She softly prayed, "Father, thank You for my new life as Mrs. Windelton. Help me to be all You need me to be so we can encourage Chad in his commitment and walk with You. May your Word be the center of our marriage." For over an hour, a fountain of praise bubbled forth from Rosie's lips. She wanted to rip open the curtains and announce to the world, "I have married my prince charming!"

Chad finally began to willingly stir. "Hey, you were beautiful yesterday, and you were more than wonderful last night! You are all I could ever hope for!" Misty-eyed and speechless, Rosie melted into her husband's arms as he showered her with tender kisses. Then with mischief in his eyes, he proceeded to unveil his surprise honeymoon agenda which he had kept a secret until this moment.

"It will take three days to drive to Disney in Florida," he responsibly explained, "so we need to hit the road."

Rosie was seized with a combination of confusing emotions. She had never been to Disney, and what a thrilling surprise this was! On the other hand, she had anticipated being in the house of the Lord together on their first Sunday as man and wife.

Rosie threw her arms around Chad and squealed, "Disney, wow! But couldn't we please attend services this morning in the church across the street, you know, our first time married? God has given us each other. It seems only right that we should begin this day honoring Him."

"No, I don't want to attend a strange church. We'll wait until we get back home. Then we'll go," Chad replied. Rosie struggled to submissively comply to Chad's decision; after all, she had studied the scriptures on submission, and she certainly did not want to usurp her new husband's leadership in spiritual matters. She trusted God to guide her husband as the head of their home. Rosie tried to hide her disappointment. Though Chad noticed out of the corner of his eye the solitary tear paving its way down her flushed cheek, he said nothing. Besides, he had designed the honeymoon, and his schedule did not provide for a church service on Sunday morning.

Rosie encouraged herself with the future dreams of their commitment to the church as husband and wife. The tear that she gently wiped from the side of her moist cheek went not unnoticed by her Comfort Angel Sapphire who swiftly caught the sliding drop in an alabaster jar marked, "Rosie's Golden Drops." Rosie would not have wanted to know how quickly the jar was soon to be filled.

## Chapter Three
# The Drunkard

Three weeks of marriage had begun to settle the Windelton's into the responsible routine of eat—work—sleep, the flip side of the story that fairy tales never pioneer. With increasing excitement, Rosie busily prepared for her new first grade class at Rosemont Elementary to begin in one week, August 30. The Illinois Department of Transportation continued to employ Chad as a surveyor networking the complicated freeway system throughout the Chicago area.

Daily the alarm rang at 5:00 a.m. with Chad returning home by 6:00 p.m. physically spent, somewhat irritable, and gluing himself to the TV for the evening's duration. Rosie contemplated the strain of labor in his eyes and the quiet, introspective stares during mealtime.

From the crack of dawn, Rosie anticipated the planning of her menu, delighting in the use of their sparkling new pots, pans, and microwave, the yet unstained dish cloths and towels, and the adventure of daringly cooking new recipes she had received with her shower gifts from close friends.

"How do you like the meat loaf?" she quizzed Chad Friday evening, hoping he was pleased with the meal. She had studied foods in school and 4-H, but for the most part, she had spent her youthful years practicing piano and flute in preparation for solo and ensemble competitions; also, she had diligently studied to obtain an Illinois State Teacher Scholarship which she was awarded her senior year of high school, so like most new brides, attending the kitchen was a new adventure.

Rosie took seriously the preparation of her meals with Chad, as she was anxious to please him in every way! Her question startled Chad from his pensive stare, and he mumbled, "It's too salty."

Rosie breathed a motionless, "I'm sorry."

"It doesn't taste like mom's," he gruffly remarked pushing the plate to the center of the table and leaving Rosie alone in the kitchen.

Her moistened eyes spilled over on to her plate as Comfort Angel Sapphire solemnly stirred to collect them. With head bowed, she whispered, "Father, please help me to become a better cook," and with that plea for assistance she began scraping the meat loaf from Chad's plate into the garbage disposal. She reminded herself of *I Corinthians 13:4, NIV, "Love is patient, love is kind,"* and rationalized that her husband was tired from a long week of work.

Meanwhile, Chad had taken a shower and was blotting cologne on his neck when Rosie piped, "Oh, where are we going tonight? Thank God it is Friday! Let's go for a movie!"

Chad proceeded to glare at his boots as he pulled them up over his feet and grunted, "I'm going out."

"I know!" declared Rosie as she bounced onto the bed beside him. "Me too!"

"No!" retorted Chad with finality in his voice, "I'm not taking you. I'm going to the bar alone." With that, he picked up his hat and headed toward the door.

"Chad, you can't do this to me! Please don't go!" Rosie's voice rose in pitch as by now she was beginning to lose composure, her vision blurring with the influx of tears barreling forth from the inner canals of her heart.

"I have to do this," he responded looking down at the floor trying to avoid the obvious pain in Rosie's eyes and face. He was like a naughty boy scolded by his father, knowing full guilt but admitting none.

Chad gripped the brass knob of the front door and in lightning speed was gone. Rosie fell in a heap and lay like a whipped dog sobbing loudly. Her chest felt like ten daggers had pierced her flesh. No consolation existed. Not even her angels were able to penetrate the shroud of mourning that enveloped her. She had no pre-existing understanding to cope with this onslaught of fearful emotions, having never seen an ounce of alcohol in her parents' home. She had no tolerance or acceptance of tavern life. She remembered that Chad had occasionally socially drunk with friends at college, but never with her.

Rosie had set down three criteria with Chad before the acceptance of his marriage proposal. Objectively, apart from all romantic emotion, Rosie knew she could not live a happy life apart from these basic lifestyle pledges from her husband-to-be:

1. No alcohol
2. Faithfully attend church
3. Attend family gatherings

Sitting on the back porch of his parents' home on a warm and billowy July afternoon, Chad had solemnly vowed to absolutely comply with these three requests. She knew that her love for Chad could cover a multitude of sins, but this criteria she requested for the assurance of her own happiness.

Since returning from Disney, two Sundays had passed, and they had yet to attend church services together. Rosie had gone alone twice, and his excuses were beginning to ring lamely in Rosie's mind.

Rosie crouched by the door as the clock struck 7 and then 8—, then 9—. Finally, Rosie awkwardly pulled herself up, splashed water in her face, then lay down on her bed clutching her Bible, with no decrease in the fountain of tears.

The clock struck 10—. She tossed about on the bed depleting the Kleenex supply. 11—still no Chad. At midnight, Rosie, calmed from utter exhaustion, drifted off to sleep. When she awoke, the light of early dawn assured the sight of Chad lying beside her in bed sleeping soundly.

"Thank You for bringing him home safely," she sighed; but, she wondered who he had been with and what he had done. Rosie didn't know how to trust God for such matters. This was new territory for her faith in hostile, unfamiliar ground. Nothing from Rosie's childhood had prepared her to handle this face-to-face confrontation with evil. She had never been in a house where the enemy roared, so this was all out of her league. Her only comfort was the innocent hope that he would never do it again. The angels pondered, but never questioned, the perfect will of God as they sealed her first, full alabaster jar. Surely, they commiserated amongst themselves, in God's abundant grace and mercy, this second jar now placed into their safe keeping would last a life time.

## Chapter Four
# First Anniversary

Rosie's bittersweet Christmas came and went unlike the stories in her stack of romance novels stashed in the back of her closet—bitter, because Chad was still bar hopping—sweet, because on the contrary, there was contentment in being a married adult and building her own family apart from her parents. Rosie held out her hand gazing at the gorgeous pearl ring Chad had placed on her finger Christmas Eve. She distinctly remembered his touching words, "I love you, Rosie, and I could never love another. I am sorry that I hurt you sometimes, and I'm sorry I've been an old grouch to live with these past few months. Thanks for putting up with me."

Chad had been her prince again that evening, embracing and kissing her, speaking tender words of deep affection; that is, until Rosie asked him to attend Christmas Eve services with her family, and with that request Chad simply replied, "No thank you," and switched on the TV. Rosie attended without him, snugly placed between her parents, but their presence could not effectually bandage her wounded heart.

On New Year's Eve, Rosie asked Chad the foolish question, "Where are you going?"

He kissed her on the forehead retorting, "Love ya!" and then walked out, leaving Rosie's female feelings a mess, vandalized like a smashed pumpkin for Father's angels to clean up. Rosie was seemingly shedding fewer tears these days, but feeling no less agony in her heart since the first night he had abandoned her at the door.

After a hard cry, she pulled out her bottom desk drawer and thumbed through Chad's old love letters written to her when he was still attending Ohio State. She deeply questioned her plight: Was she married to an alcoholic? Was her husband even saved? Was their marriage a mistake? Was she unequally yoked? These questions sent chills up and down her spine. She clutched to her bosom his precious letters filled with poetic lines of commitment and tender romance:

*I sometimes wonder how God could have created someone as wonderful and unique as you. I love you.*

*I feel that when we unite as man and wife, we will also unite in God's love. I want that, Rosie, from deep inside.*

*The desire for a life with you has recently been quite strong within me, and with that desire has come the desire to know God with you.*

*If there's one thing in this world I want to be, it's honest about religion, the belief in God and His Son Jesus.*

*Whenever I think of you and me for life, my thoughts always include a life together with God.*

*I love you, Rosie, and I want to love you and God and our life together.*

*I will try very earnestly to lead you and me in the spiritual manner which God has planned for us.*

*Like a buck with his doe, I will always be near you,*

*watching over you as you freely graze on the tender shoots of life, ever ready to protect and defend you. I love you.*

Rosie distinctly remembered the very moment Chad had given his heart to Jesus, sitting at her mom's kitchen table. She recalled the sincerity with which he prayed, and the peace that fell upon them and their relationship after that time. She had determinedly held out on his pleas for proposal until he planned to be baptized and had pledged a clean and devout life of faith as her husband. What more could she have done? Where had she gone wrong?

A part of Rosie wanted to call her mom and cry, "May I please come back home!" God's voice forbid her to do so.

~~~~~

Rosie was thankful for her bouncing first grade class of vibrant six and seven year-olds. They occupied most of her creative, emotional thinking, which really left little energy to fret over her wayward husband. The school year passed quickly, and to Rosie's surprise, summer was upon her. She had survived nine months of first-year teaching and a first-year marriage. It hadn't been easy, but she had grown and was thankful for God's faithfulness to her in supplying increased grace for each new turn she'd taken both in her teaching and in her coping faith with Chad.

"I'll be taking my vacation this summer in Michigan with my boss and some crew members for a week of fishing," Chad announced at the beginning of June. "It'll be the last week of July."

Rosie's heart leapt, "That's right before our

wedding anniversary." She wanted to scream at him, but she had learned the hard way not to raise her voice because his retaliation only increased. "Why can't we go together somewhere?" she curiously asked, but the look on Chad's face answered her. He could argue circles around her, and she knew there was no use discussing it further. Instead, Rosie signed up to serve as a counselor for a junior-high church camp at Lake Benton for that same week.

~~~~~~

"We love you!" her junior-high fan club screamed as they embraced one another and said their goodbyes.

"You were a great song leader."

"Please, come back next year!"

"Tell your husband hi from Cedric!"

"Write me!"

"Hope you miss me!"

Rosie's July 31 two-hour ride home was sentimentally sweet, like the feeling she used to have when her mom baked pumpkin pie and the family roasted hot dogs on a Saturday evening in the family room fire place. It was gratifying to be loved and appreciated for her allegiance to Jesus Christ, for the gifts and talents her Heavenly Father had invested in her. Rosie felt whole and healthy and anticipated pouring this newly stirred enthusiasm onto her husband. She returned home revived to tackle the mystery man she found herself married to.

Chad was expected home August 1, their first anniversary, and Rosie, assuming he might be tired and weary from a long trip, decided to spend her day planning a special meal for the two of them to share instead of dining out. She pulled from the cupboard the new, ivory table cloth her Grandma Black had given them for a wedding gift. Next, she placed her shiny Noritake china and tinted pink crystal. Chad had not wanted to entertain once during their first twelve months together, much to Rosie's disappointment, so she was excited about initiating the use of her tableware. Her menu consisted of Cornish hen, twice-baked potato, and her mother's favorite recipes of scalloped pineapple and broccoli casserole, topped off with Chad's mother's favorite lemon meringue pie. The meal demanded her full day of attention as she worked about the kitchen with new-found faith for their marriage. The old saying, "the first year of marriage is the worst," she hoped was true, encouraged in believing that it would surely get better from this point on.

It was 6:00 p.m. now, Rosie had expected her husband home by mid-afternoon. The Cornish hens were tenderly awaiting, and all there remained left to do was strike the match and light their wedding candle that she had reserved for their first anniversary as man and wife.

6:30 came, then 7:00—, 8:00—, 9:00—. Rosie's joy was shrinking like a balloon with a slow leak. She silently set the food back in the refrigerator, grabbed a Kleenex box, and set out to take a long walk. The full moon was beginning to rise over nearby Lake Shelby that bordered their apartment complex property. She felt like a shaken up Coca Cola can ready to explode. Ambivalent pains of fury, worry, and sorrow plagued her soul. Rosie imagined that Chad was drunk somewhere, and every ounce of newly revived faith from camp drained out of her as she walked and talked with God. Guard Angel Onyx stayed close to her side recording every word of prayer to her Father:

*Oh, God, please help me!*
*The walls of my heart are caving in*
*like an earth-quakened building.*
*My marriage . . . there is so much*
*I do not understand.*
*Coping with my husband . . . how can I?*
*The Romeo I fell in love with no longer*
*whispers Shakespeare's alluring lines.*
*Like a rat, I am trapped in a*
*cheese-appealing feast*
*that has let its latch down on me.*
*Father, if it weren't for You, I would*
*pop right out of my position as "wife."*
*Only respect for your Word keeps me home.*
*Falling out of love is an ugly reality,*
*like visiting the city dump.*
*I have tried to deny its odor*
*by suffocating my feelings,*
*but still their fumes breathe and escape.*
*All of this is ugly and stinks,*
*yet is real—really unhappy.*
*Did you dig this up*
*so I could be thoroughly cleansed?*
*Maybe you don't want garbage*
*hidden between pretty lace.*
*Praise the Lord?*
*God, how can I praise You in these*
*circumstances?*
*Please, teach me how to cope with*
*unhappiness.*
*Feeling sorry for myself?*
*Yes, I am in great need of being reached,*

*taught, and touched by You.*
*Fill me with love for my husband.*
*Please, fill me with love.*
*Jesus, the burden of my marriage*
*is like carrying 100 pound weights*
*on my shoulders.*
*Trudging slowly forward,*
*I am growing tired and weary.*
*Like a candle that has burned down,*
*I am barely flickering.*
*I don't know how I can go on,*
*but as long as my heart beats,*
*I suppose I will.*
*Your Word says,*
**"If ye suffer for righteousness' sake,**
**happy are ye." (I Peter 3:14, KJV)**
*Lord, I am not happy.*
*I would like to die. Am I going insane?*
*Please, deliver me!*

Guard Angel Onyx stood close as Rosie came to the end of herself, stopping to kneel at a stump near the water's edge. For the first time, with all of her heart, she relinquished Chad into the hands of God. She placed the care of his drinking at the feet of Jesus, then walked away, not looking back, determined in herself to leave it in Father's hands.

Rosie returned home more light-hearted and revived. There existed a new liberty in her of release and relief. For the first time since Chad had left her in a heap at their door, Rosie slept peacefully, without one sob, in the arms of Jesus. Her angels smiled as they observed the pearl of Rosie's spirit beginning to take form. Like varnish over a carpenter's hand-carved woodwork, the Holy Spirit spread a coat of righteousness over her oyster-like heart. The year was not endured in vain.

The next morning, early August second, Rosie awoke having slept like a baby. Pulling Chad's Bible from the nearby night stand, Rosie's fingers opened up the Word to **Habbakuk**, her eyes falling on **3:17-19:**

> *"Although the fig tree shall not blossom,*
> *neither shall fruit be in the vines;*
> *the labor of the olive shall fail,*
> *and the fields shall yield no meat;*
> *the flock shall be cut off from the fold,*
> *and there shall be no herd in the stalls:*
> *Yet I will rejoice in the Lord,*
> *I will joy in the God of my salvation.*
> *The Lord God is my strength,*
> *and he will make my feet like hinds' feet,*
> *and he will make me to walk*
> *upon mine high places.*
> *To the chief singer*
> *on my stringed instruments." KJV*

"This is what God has done for me," she rejoiced. "He has given me hinds' feet!" Feeling suddenly drawn to her piano, which she had hardly touched for the past year, she seated herself and began to play. Worship flowed through her fingertips, like springs of living water, as Rosie experienced the intimate presence of God. "It is well with my soul," she sang. Rosie had entered into rest. God's peace fell upon her as Angels Sapphire and Onyx pleasurably joined her in exalting their God. Had they human breath, they, too, would have harmoniously voiced sighs of relief. They were pleased with her growth.

Later, as the mid-morning sun was gleaming through Rosie's pink-lace curtains and Rosie was pulling the laundry out of her Maytag, a strong hand grasped her shoulder. Startled, she turned, and there stood a whiskered Chad. He clutched her into his arms and with intensity voiced, "I missed you so much!"

"Our anniversary was yesterday," Rosie flatly stated, leary of his intentions.

"I am sorry. I will make it up to you, I promise. Come and sit on the couch. I have something for you." He placed a dozen red roses in her arms and escorted her to the living room. "I was so miserable without you on this trip. I couldn't think of anything but you. All I could see was your face full of tears that were all my fault. Last night on my drive back home, I made a decision. I'm never going to drink again. It isn't worth the pain you go through. I can't do that to you anymore. Honey, please forgive me. I've been a rotten bum, and I'm sorry."

Rosie's heart harbored no unforgiveness, so forming the words came gently, "I forgive you."

Chad vowed, "I will never do it again," and he never did.

## Chapter Five

# The Baby Years

"Make way for the ripe water melon!" Rosie giggled as her husband carefully carried her through the threshold of their new home, designed and built by Chad.

"Maybe this little joy ride will kick you into labor," he mused as he gently rolled her cumbersome body into the Lazy Boy. Rosie, at full term, was a mixing bowl of exhaustion and elation. The spoon of circumstances was stirring up the culmination of months of construction—both within and without. This was due date, and Chad had determinedly decided to move his swollen beloved to their new, three-bedroom home. It was nestled against a timber of oak and rolling hills above Lake Sprig, three miles south of their previous apartment.

In striking contrast to their newlywed nest, Rosie perceived their new abode to be a mansion. Little did she know that the arrival of house guests—Heaven's little bundles of joy—were famous for shrinking the square footage of any dwelling place.

Indeed, that very same night, eight pound and eleven ounce, Baby Boy Andrew was born into the Windelton family. Rosie was glad God had given her the grace to attend LaMaze classes—even though alone

—and had refused to harbor resentment for Chad's unwillingness to support her in this endeavor. During hard labor, Chad held her hand, fed her ice chips, and wiped the sweat from her brow. His demonstration of care for her came in the simple and faithful manner that was her Chad, the man she cherished and knew to possess hidden caverns of wisdom and loyalty.

Rosie now took on the overwhelming task of learning how to be a mommy. She was a mother cat on call 24 hours a day, spending multiple hours in Great-grandma Windelton's old, walnut rocking chair. It had a charming creak that kept beat to her many praises to God for this package of joy delivered to their new address.

At 4 a.m. on Andrew's third-week birthday, Rosie began nursing and whispered a type of love song into his delicately formed, tiny ear:

*I do believe that my breasts*
*are your best friends!*
*You dream of their warmth through the night*
*and awaken wanting them near.*
*Your growling tummy ignites ear-piercing squeals*
*soliciting their sweet milk.*
*When tired, my breasts comfort you*
*like a soft security blanket.*
*They are your life line as you cup your*
*precious, tiny mouth around my nipples.*
*Your sucking assures me of your contentment,*
*and we both bask in the wonder of God's plan.*

Rosie squeezed her little one gently, as if babies were breakable, praying that the presence of this precious gift in their new home would tug on his daddy's heart and draw Chad back into the house of the Lord, becoming a complete family of God. It was inconceivable for Rosie to imagine facing the task of Christian training alone.

Rosie did not return to her school room that fall. How could she possibly leave her "growing sprout" in the arms of another? Surely, her heart would have broken in two had she granted her Heaven's "sprinkling-can-privilege" to the hands of a "nanny gardener."

In two years' time, Rosie's full-time homemaking expanded to embrace Baby Girl Abigail, six pounds, three ounces, only to be followed two years later by seven pound, nine ounce Baby Girl Tabitha. The quiver was filling up, and the Windelton's were abounding with personality. Chad's nest was full, as every inch was now occupied. His response was to work longer and harder hours, and even though he never changed a diaper or washed a dish, Rosie tried to be thankful for his ability to consistently go to work and return with a full day's wage. Still, the haunting question increasingly hovered over her daily activities: why won't he take us to church?

This season of Rosie's life was her most happy and most miserable. She was emotionally fulfilled as a nursing mother, lonely as a wife, and miserably overwhelmed with the daily tasks of caring for her newborn, two year old and four year old, quite certain that God had goofed in His creation process when He made woman with only two hands. On one particular afternoon when the synchronization of three little ones' schedules was simultaneously colliding, Rosie prayerfully cried out:

*My God! Why didn't You make me an octopus?*
*The walls of my home are closing in on me as my*
*children crowd around pulling, crying, whining,*
*screaming, fussing, jumping, scratching.*
*One needs a drink, another is hungry;*
*a dirty diaper here, a broken toy there.*
*I am going crazy!*
*Get me out of here.*
*My children hover around me asking,*
*"Mommy, why are you crying?"*
*I am the one who should be in the playpen.*
*My God, send me a nanny or a live-in granny.*
*How do some women have ten children?*
*I have only two hands.*
*I need tentacles to meet the needs of my little ones.*
*Lord, I want to love, not simply tolerate.*
*Pardon me, but You must have made a mistake when*
*You created mothers with only two hands.*
*How many times does my mind scream,*
*"I'm not an octopus!"*
*God, give me tentacles, ones of patience so I do not*
*erupt like a steaming volcano.*
*Calm me down.*
*Remind me of the romanticism of motherhood*
*and my eternal purpose.*
*Like a pitcher of Kool-aid,*
*I am poured out all day long,*
*and when my last drop is gone,*
*thirsty little throats continue to cry, "more, more!"*
*All of my answers lie in You.  Help me, Lord.*
*Amen.*

All of Rosie's answers did lie in God whom she loved with all of her heart. The infant days soon yielded to toddler and pre-school concerns. Day in and day out she looked to God for her strength, meanwhile observing her forlorn Chad growing more distant. During the years of Rosie's greatest need for him, he had neglected to give his helping hand, but especially her own, deep inner-self had been emotionally forsakened. Life had been too consumingly demanding to stomp a foot or command attention to herself. She had learned to take one day at a time, looking to Jesus as author and finisher of her faith. He had never let her down, even in His ability to work tender forgiveness in her heart towards her cool and aloof husband.

Comfort Angel Sapphire and Guard Angel Onyx had never left her side. They were catching fewer tears these days, as Rosie was toughening up and seemingly bearing more on her own, but they trembled to behold Chad's cool approach and estranged relationship with his children and her. They quivered in alarm at his periodic outbursts of anger and sought always to comfort the trembling heart of their beloved Rosie. One vivid testimony of God's grace was that Chad held true to his promise to never again drink. He was home and not in the bars. God's grace and faithfulness to Rosie would continue to conquer, but the angels only hoped the decrease in tears was not the indication of a hardened heart. Sapphire and Onyx knew that love never fails because they always beheld the face of their Heavenly Father, but for Rosie, Chad's disregard for her inner soul was causing the candle of love to barely flicker. After all, living with a stranger was hell**.**

## Chapter Six

# The Stranger

Rosie carefully grasped a glass in her sudsy hands, contemplating the emptiness she felt deep inside her private self. The washing machine was swishing, the drier tumbling.  Two-year old Tabitha was tugging on her legs, and four-year old Abigail was singing "Jesus Loves Me" while coloring at the kitchen table.  Six-year old Andrew was a blur, stopping at the kitchen counter just long enough to grab three, freshly-baked chocolate chip cookies, then zoom like a flash, out the back door again to conquer his world of baseball and bicycles. Rosie was gloriously surrounded with the rewarding tasks of motherhood, so why did she feel so empty inside?  Her lips gave substance to the cry of her heart as she prayerfully whispered:

*Father, when I look my husband's way,*
*a stranger meets my eye.  I don't know him.*
*I am never invited to enter his inner man.*
*I so deeply long for and desire a relationship*
*of sharing our hearts' treasures;*
*but he never lets me in.*
*He stands aloof with padlocks and boulders*
*across his heart.*
*I cannot communicate the real "me" his way,*

*so my heart grows lumpy.*
*Mostly, I feel miserable and afraid of him.*
*I am not free to express and display love for him.*
*Oh, God, this man I am married to . . .*
*I cannot get into him. He won't let me,*
*or is it that I cannot understand how?*
*Help me, please.*

"What are you muttering about in there?" Chad rudely hollered from his lounge chair strategically located in front of his TV.

With expressionless face of stone, Rosie softly replied, "I was praying."

"Well, don't be so loud. I don't want to hear it," he thundered.

Rosie's blood began to boil! Chad had rebuked her before for singing praises too loudly, and she had quieted, but this time was different. Her eyes fell to the butcher knife lying in the dish drainer. The thought of murder teased her brain; the chill of such an evil thought weakening her knees. Drying her hands, she slowly slid her body down against the cupboard next to Tabitha playing on the floor. Any defensive screaming on her part would only evoke greater retaliation from Chad. She had learned well not to throw her fuel of anger on his already fiery-hot temper. Biting her tongue, she wanted to roar like a fierce lion, yet she felt the fearful surrender of an entrapped mouse. Rosie's mind was a battlefield—the war against good and evil, right and wrong.

Suddenly, she snapped and yelled back, "I can pray if I want to!"

Fire flared from Chad's eyes, and like an agitated

dragon he contended, "Oh no, you can't! I don't want to hear it!"

"This is my home too! Whatever happened to the man I married, the praying husband you promised to be?" Rosie screamed. With that remark, Chad leaped from his chair as if electrified and lunged toward Rosie grabbing her arm, yet somewhat loosening the grip at the realization of his physical aggression. Abigail's arms wrapped themselves tightly around her trembling mommy's waist, and Tabitha's fearful crying echoed against the walls of the house.

Rosie screamed, "Get away from me. Leave me alone!" Chad's swollen nostrils resembled that of an angry bull as his breath drove hard against his family. He was out of control, in a rage. Fear quivered up and down Rosie's backbone.

"Let go of my arm, you're hurting me!" Rosie pleaded. Andrew then appeared at the door with wide eyes of innocent wonderment. Chad froze, then suddenly released his grip and exited, slamming the door with such force that the glass shattered into tiny pieces, dispersing across the porch floor. Andrew joined Abigail as they held tightly to one another, adding himself to the heap of bodies, not understanding the tragic episode that had just transpired. For many moments they tightly clung to one another. Rosie was motionless, devastated. Five minutes passed—ten minutes passed—the clock ticked on; yet, time stood still.

Eventually, Tabitha fell asleep bent over in her mommy's lap. Sweet Abigail kissed her mother and dragged her crayons and book towards her lap. She would color a pretty picture for her sad mommy and make it all better.

Andrew found a box of Kleenex and set it at his mommy's feet, and with all the manliness a six year old could muster up, emphatically stated, "I'll take care of you, mom!"

Sapphire and Onyx were absolutely beside themselves.

"We have got to do something!" Sapphire exclaimed as she held up to Onyx the nearly filled jar of freshly collected tears.

"We cannot allow this charade to continue. I'm going for help. You stay here with Rosie. I will make an appointment with General Angel." With that proclamation, Onyx departed from earth's hold.

Rosie remained motionless on the floor for over an hour. Sapphire shuddered as she observed pieces of Rosie's heart turning into stone. As much as Sapphire tried, her comfort of Rosie was not sufficient—a part of Rosie's heart was deteriorating, becoming calloused. The horror of this transformation seized Sapphire's thoughts. She had dawdled over this young woman since Rosie was first sent as a gift into the wonderful Christian home of Mr. and Mrs. Frank Hardy. Rosie's childhood had been one of innocent joy and delight. She had been parented well with loving kindness and the church as the center of their efforts. Sapphire knew God had plans for her service in His kingdom with her multiple gifts and Jesus smile. Sapphire treasured Rosie, and she bowed in reverend patience in anticipation of Angel Onyx's return report.

It was two hours later that Rosie slowly picked herself up off the floor and with Sapphire's assistance, carefully, one by one, laid her sleeping babies in their beds, then collapsed in her own. When she awoke the next morning, Chad was lying beside her.

The early morning praises of the robins caused Chad to stir. His eyes opened to behold his wife. Her auburn hair lay strewn across her satin pillowcase. Chad had always loved her hair. Her beauty caused remorse to clutch his heart, and he grabbed his chest as if a jack hammer was beating against him. He watched as Rosie's swollen, mushroomed eyes struggled to open up to the morning's light now shining through their bedroom curtains.

"I'm sorry," Chad whispered, taking Rosie into his arms and holding her scared body close to his. "I'm going to try harder to be a better husband." Rosie lay stiff and motionless in his arms, quizzing and questioning herself as to whether or not it was stupid or noble to forgive this offender. The uncertainty of her answer left a veil of hopelessness over her heart. Too many fears and too many tears had come between them.

"God, help us," Rosie prayed, and then drifted back to sleep. Chad lay in bed for the next hour holding her close and questioning the depths of darkness he was discovering in himself, quite to his inner-most, utter dismay. Why couldn't he just be the man Rosie needed him to be? Why couldn't he reach out to God and be the husband his wife desired? He would try harder—very hard—to prove himself more kind. A sincere spirit of repentance came over him as a tear trickled from the corner of his left eye onto Rosie's pillow.

Sapphire wondered why it was that Chad had no angel to catch the tear. Sapphire judged this to be perhaps a kingdom malfunction, and not bearing to see the tear wasted, swiftly added Chad's tear to Rosie's jar.

Just why was it that Chad had no assistance in his earthly walk? Sapphire dreaded to imagine that perhaps his name was not written in the Book of Life, and that his promises to Rosie and God both had only been to "please man" and to obtain the prize, his bride.

The term "unequally yoked" caused Sapphire to shiver, thinking that such had not been the divine plan for Rosie. Someone had goofed up there! Sapphire awaited the return report of Onyx. She longed to be visiting the Big City, also, but never would she leave Rosie's side. She had been her guardian since birth, and she would not leave her until both departed together when Rosie's pilgrimage was complete.

Sapphire remembered her last visit to the Big City, which, of course, had been before Rosie was born. She enjoyed earth's allegory of Heaven but sentimentally longed for Heaven's side of glory. She especially missed the emerald grass that sang praises to God continually, never needed to be cut, and always looked like new plush carpet. She would like to have seen the mansion Father was preparing for Rosie. It would surely have harps in every room! She missed the constant sweet scent of roses and the taste of spiritual fruit on all the trees that both sang and spoke continually of God's glory. In truth, Sapphire was homesick, but her loyalty to Rosie far outweighed her longing for the City. She and Rosie would return together. That is how it had been planned originally, and that plan would not be altered by any malfunction on loyal Sapphire's part.

In her love and concern for Rosie, she quietly whispered, "Onyx, please hurry!"

## Chapter Seven
# Heaven's Appointment

Guardian Angel Onyx attempted to catch a few winks on Heaven's Express, but in the twinkling of an eye, was aroused by the stimulating sensation of Heaven's breath. His ears perked to hear the greeting of that age-old familiar chorus of saints singing "Worthy Is the Lamb" and glorifying the Son of God. The sound was as one million brass horns simultaneously announcing the glory of the Almighty. Onyx could smell the sweet aroma of ten thousand varieties of roses, each emitting its own fragrance in praise to God.

Even before Onyx's eyes opened, he felt the warmth of the Son of God. His perfect light soothed Onyx's being, and his lips tasted the cool, invigorating drink from the River that flowed from the throne.

The countenance of the temple of God shone more brightly than the earth's sun, and Onyx cracked what he understood to be an earthly joke to his attendant, "Too bad I forgot my sunglasses!" to which the attending angel peered into the eyes of Onyx with questioning silence. Obviously, the servant had not yet been assigned to earth.

Onyx chuckled at his own joke and then spoke his request to the receptionist angel, "I have an appointment with The General." While he waited for

General Angel's appearance, Onyx strolled across valleys of emerald grass, ate of the fruits of joy and patience, and bathed freely in the River that rejuvenated his own spirit. He, too, shown in brilliance as his face, like a mirror, reflected the glory of God. As he basked in the warmth of the Son, he felt like an alligator that had been held captive in a Minnesota zoo. He gluttonously soaked up the pure warmth of God's love that soothed his angelic linens. Onyx was just beginning to relax in the lap of a giant, ivory lily when The General appeared.

"Greetings, my friend," his loving voice of warmth announced. Truly, love was not just a feeling in Heaven. It could be seen and touched, a tangible substance that glistened like gold.

The General took his Shawl of Love and placed it around the shoulders of Onyx, commenting, "You look weary, my friend." Onyx could not speak as he absorbed the heat of love's cloak into his angel spirit. The General watched as love melted the worry and solidified statements of earthly concern into appropriate, heavenly language of wisdom.

"Comfort Angel Sapphire and I have been with our Rosie now for 32 years. She has always been a precious jewel with much potential for service in the Kingdom of God, but her marriage is beginning to poison her spirit. We are concerned that there has been some kind of mistake. This Chad appears to be void of any assistance from our ranks. His condition is worsening before our eyes, and we are wondering just what is going on!"

The General beckoned Sapphire to enter the Library of Saints to check Chad's records. This was a very large room that resembled a Colorado mountain lined with millions of books, each bearing the name of a saint.

Onyx confessed, "We are not certain that Chad's name is in the Book of Life, although he appeared to convince us of his salvation at the time of his proposal and marriage to our Rosie."

The General made a request to his servant with precision speed, "Servant, is Chad Windelton in The Book?"

The servant vanished momentarily and returned with his nod, "Yes." Onyx was relieved, but still bombarded with many unanswered questions when the servant quietly interjected, "He is a prodigal."

The General repeated and nodded with understanding, "A prodigal." With these words, a holy hush consumed the galley, and Onyx could hear a choir of angels echoing the chilling chorus, *prodigal, prodigal, prodigal.*

The General opened Chad's book and together they watched the curtain of the great wall unveil from horizon to horizon presenting a magnified and panoramic screen of Chad's life from conception. Scenes of old passed before their eyes like a silent video in slow, forward motion. Faces and circumstances intertwined like a tapestry intricately designed. Onyx pondered God's sovereign hand within the woven needlework of just one man's life.

In humble response, Onyx asked, "Who can interpret these signs?"

It was then, the moment's memory Onyx would most treasure, that the Master Tailor appeared. A sudden gush of wind announced His presence. It was like one of earth's fall afternoons, when the leaves are rustling and the warm sun is a soothing savor, the breeze as a breath from Heaven, cool but warm, racing over the skin, tingling with refreshment and comfort.

Now, there He stood before Onyx and The General. His eyes were manifested Love, like sentimental campfires at the end of a week of camp where praise songs to God are sung, young lovers hold hands, and the warmth of friendship is celebrated. His garments shone like crystals and diamonds, bound together with pearls that live and breathe together, forming an ivory-pearl string about His waist. The brilliance was like facing World War II search lights, ten of them, three feet away! Every pearl was singing its own, unique song of praise. His hands were servitude. His feet were peace. His hair was as white silk tinted with pure gold, brilliantly illuminating each strand with its own electrical current, with power strong enough to supply a city. The General and Onyx were bolted to the ground in worship, honor, and awe of His Majesty's presence.

Jesus smiled and spoke, *Come*, and they rose as the Lord touched their robes, lifted them up, and embraced their frail figures. In so doing, they absorbed the manifest presence of God and were enabled to stand before Him and converse, much as man to man on earth. The impact of His glory had been absorbed into their own beings, and they were able to conduct Kingdom business.

With the eloquence of the universe's renowned orator, Jesus' mouth opened and spoke: *I will give substance to this Book of Life. It is not necessary for you to understand all that you have seen. Nonetheless, I will give interpretation of the parts that have bearing on your assignment with our children, Chad and Rosie.*

*I want you to understand that I sent you to watch over Rosie because she has a particular place here in my Kingdom of Heaven when her journey on earth is complete. I have need of her to minister to the millions of divorced women who return to Me shattered with abrasions to the soul, that require time and training to heal, before they are ready to receive all that I have for them in their eternal experience with Heaven.*

*It is of present grief to our Father that the universal standard of marriage is ridiculed, slandered, distorted, and mocked. The sanctity and holiness of the marriage covenant has been destroyed and ripped into shambles by the enemy's strategic attack against its holiness. The standard of the world has desecrated the holy covenant of marriage, but this was not so when Adam and Eve were created. The joining of the two was holy and precious to Us. The grievance of the current age against marital holiness runs deeply and sternly before my Father's throne. Millions of our children are returning thread-bear in spirit because of the poisonous, acidic result of divorce.*

*My Father has need of a servant to administer healing to both the brokenhearted and the cold-hearted and to those who simply learned to endure the "scab of disgrace" that ate away at their souls.*

*Beloveds, marriage on earth is holy, is holy! The spirit of man is a precious, fragile gift of my Father, sent to earth's womb to learn, to grow, and to respond to Father's love and His ministering Word.*

*The desecration of the human soul brings grief to my Father, and there is much healing needed in my saints who return amputated in soul, because of divorce's attack against their spirit man.*

*Divorce is like an acid that eats away the preciousness of the "God-likeness" invested in each soul. Divorce dismembers our children. They return to Us legless, armless, devoid of the spiritual revelation We desired for them to receive through their earthly experiences. Like a ruthless venom, divorce's snake bite kills the innocence of the soul and destroys a part of God invested in it. There is more of God in man than man realizes, for he was created in our image. It is that image which is damaged in divorce.*

*Father has need of Rosie to minister in His Chambers and assist in the instruction of the Word that will restore this chasm of soul that has been robbed and destroyed through earth's journey when its path is inevitably the one of divorce. Please, do not question my sovereignty in this marriage.* **What God has joined together, let no man put asunder***. (Matthew 19:6, KJV)*

*Do you see that saint of God?* (Jesus pointed to a wrinkled human face covering the Book of Life screen). *Her name is Sarah Windelton, Chad's great-great-grandmother. She was my servant to the little country Methodist Church that Chad's great-great-grandfather attended. This firey woman was a stick of dynamite in my late 1800's church and within her community. She was a fasting saint, and I gave her a promise that the* **"heritage of Jacob"** *from* **Isaiah 58** *would be hers. She was promised a righteous descendant in a son and grandson, a great-grandson, and a great-great-grandson. Chad is my chosen promise. I have invested in him my Spirit, and he will not always run from Me. No man's rebellion is greater than my power when intercession has made her request.*

*As you can see before your eyes, the pictures of Chad's childhood are grim. The demon of anger attached itself to the Windelton blood early in the 1900's via Great-grandfather Windelton, whose own rebellion and drunkenness opened up a nest of hornet demons that have afflicted the family. The enemy's hold has been strong in the Windelton family since then. Unfortunately, Chad was victim to his father's alcoholic frenzies and early childhood abuse. Chad remembers little of the pictures you behold, only that he feared his dad, and he, himself, has had to struggle through his entire life with the periodic visitation of hell's onslaught attack of demonic rage when his will was crossed—the curse passed on through lack of knowledgeable prayer in his ancestors.*

*Now, I take you back to the promise I made to Great-great-grandmother Windelton. This promise is mine, and it cannot be broken. The prodigal will return.*

*Please, do not question my sovereignty over Rosie's precious life and her breaking heart. I will utilize Chad as the grain of sand in her soul that will produce the eternal pearl of glory that I am in need of for Heaven's ministry. None of the tears you are collecting will go unused. I will apply them to her garment of righteousness as we prepare her for eternal work beyond my gates. When the Holy Spirit pinches the heart of man, a tear is produced. The tears will transform into healing oil of anointing that will be needed in her service to Me. No righteous suffering on earth is wasted or unaccounted for. It turns into glory in Heaven. All of earthly life is preparation for eternity's call and purpose.*

*Rosie will learn that divine purpose and destiny is accomplished not by human might and power but by the flow and the energy of the Holy Spirit Himself. It is "**not*** *by might nor by power, but My Spirit, says the Lord of hosts." (Zechariah 4:6)*

*Beloved Onyx, stay close to Rosie's side. I will send my Spirit to instruct her in my Word. There is extensive teaching I must give her. My revelation awaits her, but it will take more suffering than you care to observe her bear. The pearl will grow. Layer after layer of my divine beauty will be invested in her spirit as I work to prepare her for my Kingdom's purpose. Meanwhile, she will become an increasing blessing to her family, church, and generation as my Spirit is magnified within her and the gifts We have invested in her begin to overflow unto her world's hungry hearts.*

*Today, I send with you Wisdom Angel Narcissus, my endearing servant. He will accompany Chad from this day forth and assist you and Sapphire in your service to Rosie. We must train Rosie how to loose Chad from the chains of wickedness wrapped around him from childhood. We will reveal to her the Isaiah 58 path of fasting that Great-great-grandmother Windelton also trod. Rosie will learn to **break up unplowed ground and reap the fruit of unfailing love. (Hosea 10:12, NIV)***

*Please, do not question time. None of this growth will come naturally, but spiritually, and you know the investment of time my Father has taken in the salvation of His Bride for Me. You know the patience of God and His enduring love for even one prodigal.*

*The road will not be easy for Rosie, but I will enable her spirit to endure, and her pebbles of happiness will be exchanged for my precious stones from Heaven that will be set in her spirit as a foundation impossible for anyone to alter. She will be a tower of honor and* *intercession, an immovable rock in my church, before I place her in the assignment my Heavenly Father has granted her in our Kingdom here. By my hand I will carve in her the jewel of a **"meek and quiet spirit, which is in the sight of God of great price."** (I Peter 3:4, KJV)*

*Go now, Onyx. Take with you our friend, Narcissus, and do well the work of my ministering spirits. The day will soon come that you will return to my house with Rosie and Sapphire. Narcissus will follow later with Chad.*

*Until then, may His glory be honored and praised, and may you continue to rejoice in the everlasting blood covenant of God Almighty in my name! Amen.*

With the hush of a silent prayer, Jesus was gone, leaving His company prostrate for many moments, basking in His glory dust.

Reverently, Onyx returned the borrowed Love Shawl to The General, and the three embraced. The two angels mounted the Heaven's Express, anticipating their inspired assignment now revealed by Jesus, the author and perfecter of Rosie's faith.

No conversation between Onyx and Narcissus would be adequate preparation for the new arrival's challenging assignment awaiting them.

Most important for Narcissus was that he never lose sight of the Savior's promise, "You will return."

## Chapter Eight
# The Journal

While on the inside, God was coating Rosie's spirit with pearl and carving an imperishable jewel, the outside layers of flesh, like an onion, were beginning to be peeled away, one at a time, by the patient hand of His Lordship over her committed life unto Him.

Tough times would make one "bitter or better," and Rosie sought the better. Responding to the tug on her heart from Heaven, she began searching the Word of God for her answers, looking always to Him for the betterment of her soul through the worst of times.

Though the presence of Angel Narcissus appeared to have a calming effect upon Chad, he continued to distance himself from his wife. These were Rosie's most unhappy seasons, when she lived like a widow at the side of her husband and daily heard the tempter's voice shout, "divorce!" It seemed that daily she died one thousand deaths.

Rosie was determined that her children would not experience the terror of the raging man. Her hunger for God developed into a quiet, personal quest, as her priority became the preservation of peace in their home at all costs. Shielding her children from the expression of anger, she learned well the *Proverbs 15:1* admonition, *"A soft answer turns away wrath, but a harsh word stirs up anger."* She would be a peacemaker, believing in the ultimate harvest of her children's souls, clinging to the promise of *James 3:18, NIV, "Peacemakers who sow in peace raise a harvest of righteousness."* Her harvest of righteousness would come many years later in the faith of Andrew, the joy of Abigail, and the servitude of Tabitha.

Jesus, author of her faith, was writing volumes in her heart, some of which she began recording in a journal. These stones of revelation were the very foundation upon which God would construct her into His tower of blessing to the nations. The truth of the Word must first be proven and tried as fire in her before she could minister healing in the Kingdom of Heaven. Our service to God is eternal, though human thought may perceive Heaven as a type of resortful reward, like a Caribbean cruise. Father's kingdom never ceases. Heaven may well be a "transfer" of sorts from one geographical region to another—same Boss, same Company, but different hours and a "package of benefits" unheard of, especially housing with life assurance paid in full. Though Rosie was unaware of her future transfer, she sensed a "calling" deep in her soul, an insatiable hunger in her spirit for Him, and even this came as a gift. She knew only to pursue Him with all of her heart. Heaven had chosen her. Rosie was choosing Heaven.

### Excerpts from the Journal of Rosie Windelton

### Entry One
Last night in bed I was very grieved about the length of time it seems to be taking God to draw Chad to Him.

At 2:00 a.m. I awoke and for an instant saw standing in my bedroom doorway what appeared to be a male figure as tall as the threshold. He was all white. I sprang from the sheets, grabbed my Bible, and sat before the Lord in the living room, sensing His presence. I knew to read the third chapter of Second Peter. God comforted me in His promise that He loves Chad and is not willing for him to perish, so I must also be patient . . . I believe I saw an angel!

*"The Lord is not slack concerning His promise, as some count slackness, but is longsuffering toward us, not willing that any should perish but that all should come to repentance." II Peter 3:9.*

### Entry Two

*"She opens her mouth with wisdom, and on her tongue is the law of kindness." Proverbs 31:26.*

The "law of kindness" on my lips can bring out the best in my husband, or unkindness, the worst. The "law of kindness" is an expression of God's love to my whole family. I am a trumpeter that sounds forth the tunes of God's Spirit throughout my day. A sour note could spoil the symphony of love played in my home. Words of kindness are chords of the Spirit that can build harmony in my marriage and household.

Father, please seal upon my lips your "law of kindness" so that I might be an instrument of your peace. Amen.

*"A continual dripping on a very rainy day and a contentious woman are alike." Proverbs 27:15.*

### Entry Three

God, I resort to my pen. There seems nowhere else

to turn. Help me! There is a crazy person shouting within the walls of my saddened mind.

Like a prisoner of war, the lonely emptiness of being unequally yoked tortures me daily.

Oh, God, must I go on . . . how? I am like a boat without water, a bicycle without wheels. We are one flesh, so, in agony, I stand by his heathen ways.

God, please do something! Set me free to live sweetly within our home of blessing. Pretending to be happy is difficult for a SOUR GRAPE.

I want to be sweet clear through. From inside to outside, please sugar me!

*"Purge me with hyssop, and I shall be clean; wash me, and I shall be whiter than snow. Create in me a clean heart, O God, and renew a steadfast spirit within me." Psalm 51:7, 10.*

### Entry Four—Prophetic Word

*Beloved one, I love you. Allow Me to teach you my principle of love within your home.*

*Do not play God. This is my duty. Yours is to have a relationship with Jesus, to keep your eyes on Me—not hubby. As you give yourself to Me, I give my love to you, which in turn you give to your husband.*

*You are the light of the world, the light of your home. Your responsibility is to let your light shine upon your face in radiance, serving in gladness and willingness of mind and spirit.*

*I draw men unto Me. I save lost souls. Your part is to love—that is it—SIMPLY LOVE. I will do the rest. Amen.*

**Entry Five**

I have been studying I Samuel 25, the story of Abigail. She is an example to me of a righteous woman in a difficult marriage. She did not cower in fear towards Nabal, her husband, but was ***"bold as a lion" Proverbs 28:1,*** as she organized her servants to bring gifts and food for David and his men. I shall attempt to write her story in my own words, as she is an inspiration to me.

## *Chapter Nine*

# Abigail

**I Samuel 25**

**Entry Six**

Once upon a time, there lived a beautiful and wise woman whose name was Abigail. She lived in the far country of Maon where she and her husband owned and ruled many acres of farmland. Abigail was an exceptional woman in that she did not allow her monetary wealth to corrupt the hidden woman of the heart. Her most precious possession was an ornament of great worth, the imperishable jewel of a meek and quiet spirit which, in the sight of God, is of great price.

Abigail was a picture of dignity, a swan of character and grace elegantly afloat stilled and gentle waters. She trusted in God and never gave way to fear, for she knew that if God be for her, who could be against her?

Abigail was loved and honored by her servants. She took care to establish personal relationships with every employee in her house, genuinely prizing each servant. She was a humble woman. Often she would slip into the kitchen or housing quarters where the servants gathered, delighting in their peasant dances as well as listening to their heartaches. Her most cherished hours were spent as they shared the stories of Jehovah God and the news of their rising leader, David, of his battles being won in the mighty name of their Lord. No one doubted that Abigail loved the Lord with all of her heart, for she loved her servants as she loved herself.

Though Abigail was a picture of loveliness, this was not true of her husband. Nabal was not a kind man, he thought only of himself and did not consider the rights or feelings of anyone else, including his wife. He regarded not her physical beauty as a gift to be valued or in which to take delight, nor did his arrogant nature allow him to appreciate her sweet disposition. It was as if he wore blinders and could only see the path of his own private world. Imprisoned by introspection, he habitually withdrew into a drunken stupor.

Abigail had learned to adapt to her man, this Calebite, in loving submission both to God and him, understanding that to break their covenant of marriage could also break the heart of her God. In the early years of her marriage, the heartache had been great as she endured long months of loneliness, observing her husband turning colder by the season, but as she prayed and hoped in God, she was strangely drawn to a little group of Jewish servants who worked for her. Through their support and prayers, they helped her learn to forgive her husband. She now cried with compassion for his sinful and wicked ways, and she hoped always that God would deliver him and have mercy upon their lives as man and wife.

One morning, Abigail's prayers were interrupted when she noticed one of her beloved servants running briskly towards her. His familiar and glad-hearted smile had been replaced with an urgency in his eyes and burden in his set cheeks.

"What is it, my faithful servant?" Abigail asked with deep concern in her eyes, yet patience in her voice.

"Oh, Abigail! You've got to do something! Come

quickly! Our shepherds have been shearing sheep in Carmel, and David came and asked Nabal for some food, and David became angry with Nabal, and now he's gathering his men to attack us, and oh, Abigail, what are we going to do?" The servant shouted out in one long breath.

"Here now, beloved, calm down. Start over again and tell me the details," Abigail wisely spoke, as she placed her comforting arm around his shoulder.

Apparently, for sometime, David and his men had been in the wilderness adjoining the pasture lands of Nabal. David's men had guarded and protected Nabal's shepherds and sheep at Carmel, serving as a wall to them day and night. Nabal had, himself, come to Carmel for the sheering of his sheep, so David sent ten of his men to request food in return for the protection his army had given Nabal's men and flocks.

Indignantly, Nabal had responded with his typical arrogance, crying out, "Who is David? Who is the son of Jesse? Should I give my meat and bread intended for my own men to strangers I do not know?"

Indeed, Nabal had no regard for other men, and was so spiritually ignorant that he had no knowledge of David's chosen mission before God. He had no idea who David was!

When David was informed of Nabal's foolish response, he gathered 400 of his men shouting, "Arm yourselves with your swords! It was surely in vain that we protected all that this fellow has in the wilderness, so that he missed nothing of all that belonged to him, and he repaid me evil for good. Of all his males, not one shall be alive by morning!"

Abigail, meanwhile, made haste. Neither she nor

her servants notified Nabal, for his stubborn reputation was such that men knew he would neither receive nor listen to their pleadings. Though Abigail had always strived to sweetly submit to her husband's leadership, she had also learned to take much of his shirked responsibilities upon herself, so, with Godly boldness, she proceeded to save her house, apart from consulting Nabal.

The servants quickly responded to Abigail's gentle but urgent commands. They gathered together 200 loaves of bread, two containers of wine, five dressed sheep, five bushels of grain, 100 clusters of raisins, and 200 cakes of figs. Loading this fine food on the donkeys, they set off to meet David and his troops.

As she rode upon the donkey, her heart pounded within the bosom of a woman determined to lay down her life at all cost, even the cost of her husband's fury and, also, the humiliation she would surely feel before the highly admired and anointed man of God. As she rode, she pondered the meaning of love, praying that Nabal would later understand. She remembered their first days as young lovers, a tear now trickling down her olive cheek as she recalled those bitter-sweet days of learning how to love this man, Nabal, with God's love. Perhaps, the greatest proof of her love was about to take place.

She gracefully slid from the donkey, every nerve fiber in her body trembling with emotional excitement. She walked fearlessly towards David. Learning to live without fear in her own home had, in some uncanny way, prepared her to face boldly this demanding moment.

Now, arriving an arm's length from this so highly

honored man, Abigail fell to her knees, bowing her face to the ground. Continuing to kneel, she looked into David's eyes, and for the first time was herself a bit taken back by the presence and power of his countenance. What a comical contrast: a petite, innocent woman kneeling at the feet of a fully armed warrior! Surely, David must have felt a bit foolish, and perhaps even God, himself, chuckled.

David's ears burned as Abigail swallowed down the giant knot in her throat and pushed out what must have sounded to David like a hushed whisper:

"David, my name is Abigail. Upon me alone let the guilt of this situation lie. Please, allow me to speak with you concerning this matter of conflict between us. Nabal—he is my husband, a foolish man that has not dealt wisely with you, but I did not know of his arrogance, nor did I talk with the men you sent who requested food. I have brought provisions today for your men. Please, forgive me for this transgression against you. I know God is with you as you fight His battles and that no evil has been found in you all your days. When you become ruler over Israel and all comes to pass that has been spoken of you, then, if you forgive me, you will have spared yourself from the burden of having shed needless blood, of having avenged yourself. When the Lord brings you success and you reign as the King of Israel, I pray that you will not forget me, and that you will always remember that I have come to you today as a handmaiden of the Lord."

Abigail peered deeply into David's eyes, and accepting his outstretched hand, came to her feet. In so doing, she noticed his breast plate, dripping with tears. A tender spirit was David's, indeed. It was as she had heard he was, truly a man after God's own heart. He spoke quietly with reverence toward her unlike any voice she could recall:

"My dearest Abigail, how I praise my Lord God of Israel for sending you here today! I praise Him for your wisdom and boldness in advising me against a mistake I would have deeply regretted. Oh, bless you, dear daughter of Israel, for keeping me from avenging myself with my own hands and for spilling innocent blood. If the Lord God had not allowed you to intervene, surely, by morning, all of Nabal's men would be dead. I willingly accept your generous gifts, and I do forgive you. I pray now that you will return to your home in peace. May God abundantly bless you for your generosity to us!"

On Abigail's journey home, many thoughts flooded her mind. She didn't entertain bitterness or resentment towards Nabal. Certainly, she had forgiven him for his foolish and wicked nature and only prayed that God would touch his heart as she explained herself to him.

Well, God did indeed touch his heart, but not in the way Abigail had anticipated. As she lay the truth before him, it was as if Nabal's heart froze within him—a stroke perhaps. Ten days later, he died.

Abigail, though emotionally abused and neglected by Nabal, had never longed for this, her husband's death. In prayer, she had not sought deliverance from her husband's side. The miracle of God's love within her heart for him had kept her praying and waiting, but now, God's answer had come. He had brought deliverance.

Abigail's sincere mourning was interrupted by a request from David to take his hand, this time his hand in marriage. The warrior man of God had remembered her, as she had requested of him to do. Little did she know at that time it would be a remembrance to become his wife.

Abigail now had a new life to live, but never would she forget the joy of loving with God's love, nor the key to experiencing this love—forgiveness.

## Chapter Ten

# The Journal Continued

### Entry Seven

The story of Abigail promises me that God will deliver and reward in His own good time and plan. Her example encourages me to continue faithful to my Lord by remaining loyal to Chad. Why? Because that is my Father's "company policy" written up in His manual for my life.

Marriage is the merging of two into one, the very fiber of my likened image with God is meshed with my husband's. It is a spiritual chemistry that has taken place, the one flesh union of the bodies serving as the outward manifestation of the spiritual union.

### Entry Eight

Marriage is like a brick wall that is carefully built, one stone upon another. Mortared into the wall are children, grandparents, and all that revolves around the two lives of the couple now merged into one wall. God is the mason. The cement of His Holy Spirit works on earth to build a mighty fortress—the family—from the commitment of a man and woman. Divorce means picking up the pieces and starting all over again. It is by faith that I trust God's policy of faithfulness because I love Him and believe His Word is truth.

Who could be so bold as to take his fate upon himself? It is the fear of the Lord that confines me to His covenant wall and causes me to trust in His masonry hand more than my own to build my life as He chooses best. It is God that holds the blueprint in His hand. He foresees the end result, whereas my sight is only temporal—His, eternal.

## Entry Nine

The virtuous woman of **Proverbs 31** enjoyed the two greatest needs of her heart being fulfilled: the adoration of her husband and children.

*"Her children rise up and call her blessed; her husband also, and he praises her. Many daughters have done well, but you excel them all. Charm is deceitful and beauty is passing, but a woman who fears the Lord, she shall be praised." vs. 28-30.*

A woman is designed to need the praises of her husband and children. If I am indeed a woman who reverently and worshipfully fears the Lord, then certainly God will see to His business of bringing me praise. He has promised! I will absolutely reap the rewards of faithfulness.

Lord, help me to be an Abigail. If I am a woman that fears the Lord, I WILL BE PRAISED!

## Entry Ten

Father, I cry out to You over and over as I yearn to be understood.

There swirls deep within me a reservoir of feelings, ones I try to avoid, but they rise up like a tyrant whirlpool.

I keep whispering, "God, oh God," hoping for deliverance. Despite the inner turmoil and confusion, I keep trusting in You, but I hate the unrest that hides in my soul.

There is a hollowness in my hidden person, and it *mourns continually* for my marriage.

Oh, God! Am I such a poor example of your abundant life? Open my husband's eyes that he might see—You. Amen.

*"Rivers of water run down from my eyes, because men do not keep Your law." Psalm 119:136.*

### Entry Eleven—Prophetic Word

*"Let your fountain be blessed, and rejoice with the wife of your youth. As a loving deer and a graceful doe, let her breasts satisfy you at all times; and always be enraptured with her love." Proverbs 5:18-19.*

*It is the marriage bed that is undefiled. What transpires between husband and wife is holy and undefiled. A man's pleasure is his woman's body. She is to be a tower of perpetual honor and pleasure unto him, one that he can ascend and reign as king upon. His tower is adorned with the fragrance of a garden, a sweet smelling perfume that beckons him continually. One taste of her ointments satisfies momentarily. The sweet ecstasy of her ascent yields only to more desire of her beauty.*

*Her breasts belong to him and only him. They are his reward and pleasure, my escape for him to pleasure in.*

*Husband, you shall be always ravished with her love, easily wooed from the world's voice into her arms of sensitivity and warmth. She is your retreat of honor.*

*There within her you are lord of the castle; 'tis your domain, your authority.*

*Beloved, recognize my gift to you in your woman's body. She is to be unto you the scent of one thousand roses. Her petals are yours to bask in, like a bed of flowers specially chosen and picked for you.*

*Your bed chamber is holy unto Me. Your union is sanctified, and my oil from heaven drips upon your kisses.*

*Tender and gentle is my atmosphere of love, like two doves cooing in morning's breeze. Like a raging river, passion's zeal announces its power of devotion and proclaims its ownership of love.*

*Husband, strum her body's strings as a harp from Heaven. Make melody upon her keys and cause the praise of marital love to ascend to my throne. Your union is holy—is holy—is holy unto Me! Amen.*

### Entry Twelve

*"A continual dripping on a very rainy day and a contentious woman are alike." Proverbs 27:15.*

Father, help me not to be a quarreling and bickering nag to Chad; but, rather, a blessing, that he might REJOICE with the wife of his youth!

### Entry Thirteen

*"For three things the earth is disquieted, and for four which it cannot bear . . . an odious woman when she is married." Proverbs 30:21, 23, KJV.*

"Odious" in the Greek means unloved. The *NIV* reads, *"an unloved woman when she is married."*

Father, I thank You that Chad loves me, that he is a loyal and faithful husband. Help him to learn to open up and be free to express and enjoy his love for me.  May I always be able to say, *"I am my beloved's, and his desire is toward me." Song of Solomon 7:10.*

## Entry Fourteen

Father, my marriage is like a giant jig-saw puzzle with pieces haphazardly strewn about.  I am like a widow living with a haunting skeleton, but I am not going to give up!

With your patient hand, please piece us together so we will share a sweet closeness.

Father, You know your business.  You are a master in placing shattered pieces of lives back together.

Chad and I made a holy covenant before You, our Heavenly Father, vowing to remain faithful to one another.

Your Holy Spirit, in return, promised to "super glue" us into one and keep our lives together as man and wife.

I will not break covenant!  Thank You for cementing together our lives, even though You appear to be working ever so slowly!

I place all of my trust in You to enrich our marital harmony by your grace.  Amen.

## Entry Fifteen

A friend told me today that her divorce was like setting one bag of problems down as she walked out the door, only to pick up another bag.  She is now happily married to a devout Christian man, but her first husband has since been saved and attends church with his new wife's family.  I think I would find it hard to live with myself under those circumstances.

## Entry Sixteen

I observe a *bittersweet joy* in my friend's second marriage because of the straining consequences of a broken home. The ending of a marriage is the severing of one flesh, most surely like the shredding of muscle, with precious and innocent children, friends, and grandparents in the middle.

God, I don't want that for Andrew, Abigail, and Tabitha. Please, work your miracle healing between Chad and me. Amen.

## Entry Seventeen

*"But if the unbeliever departs, let him depart; a brother or a sister is not under bondage in such cases. But God has called us to peace." I Corinthians 7:15.*

Father, I understand that You would not approve of physical abuse or adultery, but Chad and I have neither of these in our marriage. We are just unhappily incompatible. Crankiness is not grounds for divorce! He can choose to leave me, and I would be free, but Chad loves me—in his own way. Help me to love him. I know he will return to you—someday. Just please give me the patience to wait!

## Entry Eighteen

*"Then Jesus said, Father, forgive them, for they do not know what they do." Luke 23:34.*

I must forgive and keep on forgiving! I must love Chad for who he is and FORGIVE him for what he is not.

## Entry Nineteen

Lord Jesus, as I stand scouring pots and pans, I

marvel at the new peace and joy that also shines deep within me. I am glimmering proof of your Holy Ghost scour!

How can I ever thank You for the amazing cleansing you have done in my wicked heart?

Content to lay down my life, I serve my husband not wanting to run away from home, murmur against decisions, or cry in self-pity.

You have pruned me back to a bunch of nubs. I screamed when You cut, but now I can rest. Amen.

## Entry Twenty
*"I hate divorce, says the Lord God of Israel." Malachi 2:16, NIV.*

Dear Father,

I have lived with my man out of lawful obedience to your Word. Knowing I must not violate covenant in divorce, I have *hung in there* out of loyalty to You.

You have gently chastened your daughter using this rock and hard place, for I am like a young filly that You have broken. Now, I am willing to yield to your reins.

I want to manifest your Lordship by honoring and loving my mate, just *"as Sarah obeyed Abraham, calling him lord." I Peter 3:6.* I must love my husband, but I cannot manufacture this precious gift myself.

I come to You believing I shall receive because I ask in the name of Jesus. My hands reach out to You as tears slide down my cheeks. Weakly, I admit that I want to do things your way.

I wait on You, Lord, remaining still and knowing that You are God. I wait on You.

Love always,
Your Broken Filly

### Entry Twenty-One—Prophetic Word

*"No one can come to Me unless the Father who sent Me draws him." John 6:44.*

*When your light grows dim, then so does my drawing power within you.*

*When my Spirit resides in you, it longs to manifest itself through the light of your life. If my Spirit is quenched within you, a mere glimmer gets through to the dark world.*

*Let your light shine in your home, with your family, not allowing the enemy to steal, kill, or destroy. This is your battle, to defeat Satan using the name of Jesus as your defense.*

*The enemy would like to blow out your light so there would be no drawing power in you calling upon your husband's heart.*

*Do not allow the burdens and frustrations to crush your spirit. Resist the devil, and he will flee. Run to Jesus for your needs and protection. He will pick you up before defeat and will restore within you the glow of His goodness.*

*Wager not time within your calculating mind. Again, I am God, not you. The enemy would have you being concerned with your labor in terms of months and years. Resist such tempting thoughts.*

*Live one day at a time unto Me. If I choose your lifetime to draw one man to Me, then it is best, my will, and your rewards will be immense, running over in plenty. Amen.*

## Chapter Eleven
# Golden Thread of Grace

It had been three years since Wisdom Angel Narcissus' arrival. During this time, Rosie had spent endless hours digging into the Word, and she was beginning to know peace as well as seeing the labor of motherhood bring fruitfulness in her budding children. Andrew was now a sprouting fourth grader, with Abigail in second, and Tabitha beginning kindergarten.

The Father was pleased with Rosie's growth. As God's plan for her family began to unfold in Rosie's heart, it appeared, also, that Chad seemed pleased to peacefully dwell at his wife's side, though withdrawn and somewhat distant, he chose daily to remain faithful to his wife and provide for his family.

Chad seemingly made no earth-shaking testimonies of change; although, it did appear to Rosie that God's promise of sanctification in her husband's heart was slowly taking place. The razor-sharp edges of his personality were piercing less and less and being smoothed by an unseen Master of Trade. Rosie clung to the promise of *I Corinthians 7:14*, *that the unbelieving husband is sanctified by the believing wife, and their children are holy*.

It was August 26. Rosie was taking the traditional Windelton *first day back-to-school* picture, with all three children decked out in new outfits, shiny backpacks, unsmudged Nikes, and innocent excitement.

They had their morning devotions together at the breakfast counter, brushed their teeth, kissed their mommy good-bye, and swiftly ran out the door to catch the 7:30 bus. Rosie was left alone in their tracks, pondering the miracle of her "grown-up" family. Tears swelled in her eyes as gratitude to her Father erupted from the deepest caverns of her motherly heart. Jesus authorized the crystallization of thought into creative word, and Rosie was blessed in recording the divine moment to be forever cherished:

### *Golden Thread of Grace*

*Baby's out of diapers.*
*Plastic pants are thrown away.*
*The rocking chair is resting.*
*The tribe's at school today.*
*The toys are stacked in piles*
*right where they're to be found*
*by the same sets of hands*
*that used to only stroll them 'round.*
*I can see my carpet!*
*(They straightened up the house!)*
*I hear the wall clock ticking.*
*Things are quiet as a mouse.*
*What happened to the days*
*when the only rest I knew*
*was to climb into the playpen*
*in refuge from the crew?*
*Perhaps I'm only dreaming.*
*No, I pinch myself amazed.*
*My prayers were heard and answered.*
*I survived the toddler days!*

*Those were times of endless giving,*
*wiping noses, tying shoes.*
*The "supernatural octopus"*
*learned her P's and Q's.*
*Now suddenly it seems*
*those days are in the past.*
*Though I never thought I'd say this,*
*"It seems they've slipped by fast!"*
*Now with sentimental fervor,*
*I can romantically recall*
*eggs broken on the floor*
*and crayon marks scribbled on the wall.*
*These are precious days*
*with my children growing tall,*
*subtraction and division,*
*gymnastics and football.*
*The wisdom of a mother*
*is to savor every season,*
*that in everything with God*
*there is a purpose and a reason.*
*A mother has the privilege*
*of sowing daily seeds,*
*watering with patience*
*and praying out the weeds.*
*Every day is priceless*
*when we garden with His love;*
*and when becoming weary,*
*gaining new strength from above.*
*We should strive to not be hurried*
*when each new day arrives,*
*but carefully cherish*
*our children's precious lives.*
*Each new day is special.*

*We need to hold them dear,*
*being thankful for these days*
*we can have our children near.*
*God's greatest call for mothers*
*is surely that we learn*
*to teach our children*
*how to love God in return.*
*On our knees before the Lord,*
*praying mothers all receive*
*a "needle of love"*
*that inspires children to believe.*
*From birth we sew unceasingly.*
*'Round our children's hearts we lace*
*God's most important stitch—*
*His **Golden Thread of Grace.***

## *Chapter Twelve*
# Bruised Heart

"Yum! Fried chicken, my favorite!" Andrew shouted as he sprinted past the kitchen table like a blur, as was the usual case, flying 100 miles an hour in youthful pursuit of a ball game or neighborhood friends at the door. Andrew was a marvel to Rosie. Today was his twelfth birthday, and Rosie wondered where the years had gone. He stood now shoulder to shoulder with her, beaming with pride that he could match his mother in height, striving always to equally beat her in wit and cleverness. He was a *little Chad* in body but not in soul. Rosie recalled the many nights she had knelt at his bed and claimed her Father's promise of sanctification over her children, particularly Andrew. She had dealt with the arrogant pride, strong will, and anger that manifested often as a young child and a willful grade schooler. She had broken the curse of the generations over her children, and through the powerful blood of Jesus Christ, she had stood in the gap for her son and daughters, claiming what was legally hers in Jesus.

Andrew was a living testimony of the grace of God. His gangly arms wrapped themselves around Rosie's shoulders, "You're a good mom!" he assured her as he gave her an awkward but firm and loving squeeze. "Now, when do we eat?"

"I'm stirring the gravy now. Call your sisters and dad," Rosie pleasingly responded to her son's hunger cry. As Andrew gathered the crew for his birthday meal, Rosie hustled about the kitchen. Abigail poured the drinks, and Tabitha handled the ice duty.

The hustle-bustle screeched to a halt as Rosie reached her hand to grasp Andrew's. Andrew's hand, in turn, clutched Abigail's, and Abigail nestled her slender hand into Tabitha's. Rosie paused, hopefully waiting for Chad to join hands with his family; but, instead, he grabbed the serving spoon and clamored into the mashed potatoes, scraping the side of the bowl, and sending a discomforting chill up and down Rosie's spine. He continued to ignore her many pleas to join them in meal-time prayer. As he proceeded to serve himself first, appearing oblivious to four sets of pleading eyes his direction, Rosie and the children bowed their heads and in a sweet harmony spoke: "Before we eat, we bow our heads, and we thank You, Lord, for this daily bread, in Jesus' name. Amen."

Wisdom Angel Narcissus stabbed Chad's heart with his sword, but its hardened core was, as usual, impenetrable. Angel Narcissus shook his head as both Comfort Angel Sapphire and Guardian Angel Onyx gave glances of irritation to Chad. Since Narcissus' assignment to the prodigal, he had not gained any significant ground with him. Chad had grown accustomed to that piercing feeling of conviction, but the sword's tip only triggered a defense mechanism of angry justification in his thoughts. Narcissus longed for a glimpse of repentance and unceasingly worked nobly towards that effect in Chad.

Andrew mounded his plate with a double helping of mashed potatoes and gravy (having made certain they were not the flake kind), and as he reached for the salt, his elbow tipped over his glass of milk.

"Now, look what you've done!" erupted Chad. "Twelve years old and you are still spilling your milk!" Rosie leaped from her chair to seek cloths for wiping up the spilled milk, and the girls cowered down in their chairs at their father's angry outburst. Andrew became bright red, embarrassed and humiliated, once again, by the hands of his father's inappropriate temper.

"I didn't mean to," Andrew quietly confessed.

"You always ruin everything!" Chad bellowed, and with that crude rebuke, he thrust his plate forward, initiating a domino effect against the remaining table wear, knocking over the salt, the vase of fresh carnations, and the bowl of green beans onto the carpet, leaving behind a worse mess than Andrew's spilled glass could have ever made.

Rosie's face froze like stone, her heart being torn into one thousand pieces, each piece screaming its own sermon of rationale, defense, and pleas to Chad. Six little eyes of youth watched her for cues as to how they should handle this uncomfortable situation. Not one tear fell from her eyes.

Angel Sapphire held out her alabaster jar, actually hoping that Rosie would tender-heartedly respond to the circumstance, but no, there were no tears, not a thread of emotion left in her. She felt dead inside, like a carcass lying in the middle of the road—or she wished she could be.

Tabitha scurried to her mommy's side and sweetly hugged her. Abigail quickly followed suit, and Andrew's words sought to comfort her with, "Mom, I didn't mean to ruin everything. I'm sorry."

The four hovered together in the aftermath of abuse, victimized by an enemy they were supposed to love and honor. No sanity existed in that moment, only an onslaught of confusing feelings and questions that seemed unanswerable. Quickly, the four settled back into the meal. Dad had done it again—ruined a special occasion. Rosie tidied up the table, and the four silently resumed eating. Rosie tried with all of her gumption to smile and "make it up" to her three precious treasures. Yet, in the deepest caverns of her heart, she was miserable and desperate for relief from the hideous lifestyle she endured.

After cake, ice cream, and gifts, Rosie excused her children, desiring to be left alone to contemplate their plight. Andrew ran down to the park with his new football in hand, Abigail rode off on her Schwinn bicycle, and Tabitha curled up into a ball on the couch and fell asleep, leaving Rosie alone with the dirty dishes. Disturbing thoughts began to tear at her nerves:

*People can understand a bruised arm or a blackened eye, but how could one explain a bruised heart or a blackened soul? Intangible, but devastating as a hurricane's rage is the merciless poison of depression. My soul in defense can either strike out like a cornered tiger or withdraw into hiding like a fleeing mouse. The bold tiger might be struck down or the shy mouse shrivel up, both ending in lifelessness. God, what answer have You for the vicious circle of abuse? What hope is there for the one ensnared by the arms of a wicked man?*

## *Chapter Thirteen*
# Circle of Abuse

Rosie's hands began to methodically move through the mountains of pots and pans, but her thoughts were elsewhere, far away, as she pondered the faithfulness of God and the hopelessness of the abusive circle. Her inability to alter or change her circumstances was mind boggling. Even in the midst of devout prayer, she retreated bruised and maimed in soul. Hot water ran over Rosie's hands, filling the sink with sudsy water as she cried out to God.

*What hope is there for such a woman as I? For adultery or beatings, a woman would or should pack the bags, but for scars in the heart tissue, who can plead? Where is your vengeance?*

Rosie's tear ducts were painfully swollen, one single tear now trickling from her right eye. Guardian Angel Onyx quickened the alabaster jar, and he nodded to Comfort Angel Sapphire, relieved that Rosie was introspectively examining herself with new emotion. They beckoned the Holy Spirit to bring her comfort and revelation as she deeply pondered the condition of her soul before her Lord.

*How am I to ever trust a purring cat that knowingly transforms into a cougar with long, sharp claws upon provocation? How can it ever be possible for my womanly heart to invest itself in this man? Always the deal reneges. Always I am bruised and beaten by scornful words of wrath that break not the skin of my flesh. They only silently and secretly mutilate the lining of my soul where no man sees or understands the hurt, the pain, nor the recovery.*

*How can such a relationship of terminal abuse be justified? How can I ever expect happiness? For within this curse of double standards lies a hopelessness, growing like an undiagnosed cancer, with teeth ready to gnaw to extinction every cell of goodness and love between us.*

*How can I again possibly trust my abuser, knowing that potential for violence the "transformer" possesses —not to mention his own lack of noted repentance toward God and toward me?*

*I cannot even cry out in defense for fear of being scorned and rudely tossed again into the fire. My words of accusation are intolerable to his ears. They incite rage and fire in his eyes.*

*I am destined to become the fool of all fools, imprisoned by a silent enemy that is only a lie's fear. The imprisonment of my soul to increasing degrees drives a wedge into my heart, one of fearful carefulness and hopelessness. Fear is not of God. But one learns not to throw gasoline onto a fire. And so it is feared respect that freezes my best intentions—and the abuser goes free. For within the circle of abuse, there is no escape.*

*God, I find no answers in your Word for me in this*

*abusive circle. Somehow "forgive" is not strong
enough solace nor ammunition.*

*I have no hope apart from your deliverance. And
the irony—the ridiculously hideous thinking of the
abused is: what am I doing wrong?*


That unnerving question fell upon Rosie like a
heavy boulder, dropping her to the floor. Like a
deflated balloon, she lay in a crumpled heap, oblivious
to her surroundings. This heart-rending plea was
bringing microscopic clarity to the introspection of her
life. The question "what am I doing wrong?" loosened
the long time, bottled-up hurt, causing tears to gush
forth from deep within the hidden-most caverns of her
inner being. Waves of emotion beat against her heart as
she pondered the question at hand.

Onyx and Sapphire hovered over Rosie and spoke
forth the Word of God in her behalf.

Onyx: *"Hope deferred makes the heart sick . . ."*
*Proverbs 13:12.*

Sapphire: *"A merry heart does good, like medicine.
But a broken spirit dries the bones." Proverbs 17:22.*

The intensity of Rosie's sobbing peaked.

Onyx: *"The Lord is near to those who have a
broken heart, and saves such as have a contrite spirit."*
*Psalm 34:18.*

Sapphire: *"The Spirit of the Lord is upon Me . . . to
heal the brokenhearted . . . to set at liberty those who
are oppressed." Luke 4:18.*

Rosie weakly began whispering the sweet name of
Jesus repeatedly.

Onyx: *"Heal me, O Lord, and I shall be healed;
save me, and I shall be saved, for You are my praise."*

*Jeremiah 17:14.*

Sapphire: *"By this I know that You are well pleased with me, because my enemy does not triumph over me." Psalm 41:11.*

Rosie's voice steadied, and her cry of "Jesus!" intensified.

Onyx: *"What then shall we say to these things? If God is for us, who can be against us?" Romans 8:31.*

Sapphire: *"Surely He has borne our griefs and carried our sorrows . . . the chastisement of our peace was upon Him; and by His stripes we are healed." Isaiah 53:4-5.*

With her hands cupped in worshipful surrender, Rosie received the healing touch of Jesus.

The Holy Spirit of God enveloped the *wilted Rose* with His omniscient presence, and with the assistance of Onyx and Sapphire, they wove a holy robe of righteousness around her spirit. The hand of the Spirit of God lined her spirit with a fresh layer of shining pearl, **and the peace of God that passes all understanding rested upon her to keep her heart and mind in Christ Jesus her Lord. (Philippians 4:7)**

Onyx and Sapphire began singing high praises to God, and the Holy Spirit strummed Rosie's heart like His lyre, ministering to her sweet verses of praise and comfort. This was a holy moment, a divine visitation. Father's daughter cried out to Him, and He sent His Comforter to minister an increment of increased grace into her heart and life. Rosie's very blood began to flow with an increase of zeal, wit, and will to conquer the foe and instigator of evil. Her limp petals quickened with strength from the revitalizing River of Life.

Rosie's lips began to quiver, and then, like the

bursting forth of a dam, praise to God flooded freely from the very depths of her spirit.

*I love you, Lord, and I lift my voice . . .*
*Amazing grace how sweet the sound . . .*
*I exalt You, oh, Lord . . .*
*It is well with my soul . . .*

It was at this destined moment that Rosie's alabaster jars of tears were transformed into a sweet perfume by the addition of her Father's tear. Her broken will had gripped her Daddy's heart. His response was the tear drop of anointing, an oil of given grace for her to abide in His presence unceasingly as a gift of worship unto Him. The lifestyle of brokenness had elicited her Father's favor.

Rosie's body began to stir. With Onyx on her left side and Sapphire on her right, they began to elevate her arms. Her surrender to God was perfected in her worship of Him. She had triumph over the forces of evil. She was more than a conqueror through Jesus Christ. Greater was He within her than he that was in the world.

Onyx exclaimed, ***"Behold, the Lord's hand is not shortened, that it cannot save; nor His ear heavy, that it cannot hear." Isaiah 59:1.***

Sapphire proclaimed, ***"And the God of peace will crush Satan under your feet shortly." Romans 16:20.***

Rosie's angels assisted her in rising from the floor. From her encounter with God, she would forever and eternally be changed into her Father's *sweet perfume of worship.*

## Chapter Fourteen
# The Plan Unfolds

Two years later . . .

Rosie drowsily stirred beneath the handmade quilt that had been sewn with love by her Grandmother Hardy. Her early-morning, puffy eyes focused in on the alarm clock's blurred arms—three o'clock a.m. She sat up straight in bed, stirred by a strange churning in her spirit.

"What, Lord, what is it?" she gently questioned as she slid over Chad's still body and slipped her feet into her pink-cushioned slippers. As she wrapped her house coat about her chilled shoulders, her trembling hand grabbed for the maple bedpost. Rosie steadied herself, surmising that perhaps she had risen too quickly, and then quietly proceeded down the hallway.

In the kitchen, Rosie prepared the morning pot of tea and clutched her Bible to her chest. "Father, who am I to pray for?" Rosie asked, assuming, as like many times before, that she had been awakened from her sleep to specially intercede for a person or situation.

Angels Sapphire and Onyx stood at each side, ready to assist in their Lord's commands, while Rosie's concentration was disturbed by an increasing aching in her head. She sauntered over to her calendar and checking dates she muttered, "There is no good time for a headache." With increased voice, Rosie announced, "It is written: *my healing shall spring forth speedily!*" *Isaiah 58:8.* She then placed her head face down into the palms of her hands, resting them upon the dining room table. After a few moments, Rosie's face lifted, and she looked up, fixing her eyes on the family portrait of Andrew, Abigail, and Tabitha. As she prayed for her little darlings, praise flowed from her lips, and her Lord responded with His intense presence falling upon her like a blanket of holiness, as if a heavenly fog had settled in the room. Rosie became motionless, sensing God's nearness, her tears flowing freely, ones of joy. Angel Sapphire approvingly caught her joy drops.

Rosie reverently listened to her Father whisper, "Beloved, I love you! You will be coming home soon." Rosie had heard this many times before, remembering that in God's sight, *"One day is as a thousand years and a thousand years as one day." 2 Pet. 3:8.* She longed for the moment she would see Jesus face to face and be tightly embraced by her Father's arms.

Rosie basked in this phenomenal morning. God was good, and He was gracious to manifest Himself to her at such a time as this. Too soon, the alarms began ringing, and Chad was up and gone to work. Grandma Windelton arrived at 8:00 a.m. to pick up the girls for an overnight stay, and Andrew was shooting baskets in the driveway, preparing for his school basketball tryouts coming up in three weeks.

It was close to 9 a.m. when Rosie noticed a strange and demanding pounding in her head. Her hand reached up and pressed itself like a cushion against her left brow. Feeling dizzy and nauseous, she fell on the couch. After a few minutes, she stabilized, then carefully guided her feet towards her bedroom. In hand was a grocery list a mile long, and she wanted to shower before leaving home.

As Rosie grabbed her clean clothes from the closet, the intensity of pain again increased, and her vision blurred. She was beginning to feel slightly disoriented and emotionally flustered. Tears welled up in her eyes, and she sauntered toward the bathroom.

Andrew brushed against her in the hallway and noticed her tears, asking, "Mom, what's wrong?"

"Oh, nothing, dear. I'll be all right. I just kind of have a headache," she softly replied, almost breathlessly void of expression.

Andrew didn't like the look in his mother's eyes nor her stumbling pace and the sound of her voice. He had seen her cry before, and he understood, in part, his dad having something to do with her tears; but, this was different. He had a disturbing feeling inside of himself that he had never experienced before.

"Mom, I think I'd better call dad."

"No! Really, I'll be fine!" She scooted him out the bathroom door and locked it behind her.

Andrew determinedly called his dad at work, then paced the hallway, listening carefully to any sounds he could detect. One time he heard an alarming thud and he screamed, "Mom, are you alright?"

Rosie had slipped in the shower, but grabbed hold of the rail and lifted herself back up.

"I'm okay," she called out wearily. Andrew was then even less assured of her "okay" state of being. He paced up and down the hallway until he heard his dad's Ford Bronco pull into the drive. In a split second, Andrew was out the door.

"Dad, something's really wrong with mom!" Andrew frantically screamed. In response to the urgency in Andrew's commanding voice, Chad's face froze in a terror that Andrew had never before seen in his father.

Dropping his papers in hand, Chad ran to the door shouting, "Where is she?"

"In the bathroom, but the door is locked!" Andrew yelled. Chad cursed and his heart rate doubled.

"Rosie! Rosie! Are you okay?" Rosie couldn't hear his call. She was sinking deeper and deeper into a silent depression of frenzy and pain. The shower was running, but her body was writhing with something that felt to her like increasing electrical shocks. Rosie's head was cracking up inside, like fireworks going off in her brain. The roar between roars was crescendoing, but then suddenly diminished as her grip on the door bar loosened.

"Oh, my God," she whispered, "help me!" With that last cry, her hand relaxed, and she fell into a crumpled heap onto the shower floor. An unnerving, crashing sound escaped through the door.

"Rosie! Rosie!" Chad frantically yelled. Andrew was crying with a deep fright that he had never known before. Without further thought, Chad's leg thrust itself through the door, and he bolted in. Forcefully pulling open the shower door, he blared, "Oh my God, oh my God! Rosie, what's happened?"

"Daddy, daddy, what's wrong?" Andrew screamed frightfully, hysterically asking, "Is she dead . . . is mom dead?"

Chad grabbed some towels and hollered to Andrew to call 911. Andrew bravely pulled himself together enough so that his fingers could shakingly punch in the numbers. His voice quivered loudly as he requested help.

Chad held Rosie's limp body in his strong but trembling arms, and for the first time in Andrew's life, he heard and saw his dad praying. "God, oh God, please don't let Rosie die!" Chad's eyes were swelling with rivers of tears, too caught up in his own fearful grief to notice Andrew's horrified emotion.

The five-minute wait seemed like five hours to both of Rosie's men. Finally, Andrew wrapped his jittery arms around his mother and dad, and father and son wept together. Suddenly, from deep within Andrew's born-again spirit, words rose up through his lips, and a voice that became audible spoke prayerfully. "Father, please help mom. Don't let her die. I love her so much. She means everything to me. Please, don't let her die. Please, come now and heal her! In Jesus' name." Then softly, but with heroic boldness, Andrew began to recite the *Twenty-third Psalm*:

*"The Lord is my shepherd: I shall not want."* With his face pressed into his dad's shoulder and his hand on his mom's arm, his voice, though shaky, recited each word slowly and distinctly.

*"He makes me to lie down in green pastures; He leads me beside the still waters."* Chad's head was bowed against Rosie's chest as his tears streamed onto the carpet.

*"He restores my soul; He leads me in the paths of righteousness for His name's sake."* Andrew's words pierced his daddy's heart as he shamefully listened to his little man of God cry out for help.

*"Yea, though I walk through the valley of the*

*shadow of death, I will fear no evil; for You are with me; Your rod and Your staff, they comfort me."* Chad remembered watching Rosie sit around the dining room table conducting devotions with his children and teaching them to memorize *Psalm 23*. The scorn he had felt towards Rosie at the time was now transformed into a sharp wedge that was hammering deeply into his soul.

*"You prepare a table before me in the presence of my enemies; You anoint my head with oil; my cup runs over."*

"What a fool!" Chad shamefully muttered to himself. A distant siren pierced the stillness of the room between Andrew's words.

*"Surely goodness and mercy shall follow me all the days of my life; and I will dwell in the house of the Lord forever."*

The two-edged sword had slain the dragon . . . out of the mouths of babes and sucklings. Chad's frozen grip on his wife's limp body was loosened by the gentle, but persuasive hands of the EMT.

Andrew rode in the front of the ambulance while Chad stayed at Rosie's side in the back. Andrew never took an eye off of his mother's pale face as he kept crying, "God, oh God, help my mom!"

At the hospital, Dr. Edward Charlesworth explained to Chad that Rosie had endured a stroke. In the brain there had developed a blood clot. The family could see Rosie, but she would be closely monitored because of the danger of the blood clot swelling and causing further complications.

Rosie's eyes filled with tears as she heard Andrew's words at her bedside, "Mom, I was so afraid we had lost you. You're the greatest mom ever. I love you, mom,

I love you!"

Chad held Rosie's hand after Grandpa Hardy took Andrew home to spend the night with him. "Rosie, I love you. I am here for you, babe."

Rosie couldn't move or speak but could only weakly squeeze Chad's hand.

By 9:00 that evening, Rosie's condition had stabilized, and she was quietly resting. For the first time since Rosie's stroke, Chad was left alone with his introspective thoughts. Wisdom Angel Narcissus was at his side encouraging his repentance throughout the evening.

Nurses monitored Rosie's vital signs every 15 minutes and urged Chad to leave and get some nourishment and rest, but he refused. He was glued to her bedside and would not take his eyes off of her. A strange, prevailing fear was growing in his belly. Agonizing blasts of dynamite were exploding inside of his heart chambers, like steady intense bombs bombarding his thoughts and heart.

Every possible human emotion wrestled within him as his soul experienced flashback after flashback of Rosie and their marriage—her gentle, soothing smile and his stubborn mule responses to her. Chad was surged with sudden remorse, stabbing him painfully and regrettably.

His thoughts were waves of guilt pounding his brain as he watched his beloved's chest weakly moving up and down, her soft auburn hair tossed across her pillow. How many times had he ignored her needs? How many times had he looked the other way, but now, he couldn't take his eyes off of her?

"This is my fault," he groaned. "I put you under too

much stress . . . I asked too much of you . . . I was unreasonable with you."

Chad took Rosie's hand and her eyes opened. She observed his misty eyes and listened to words she had waited seventeen years of marriage to hear.

"Babe, I am sorry for being bad to you. Forgive me for being a jerk, a rotten bum all of these years. Please, don't leave me. You've got to get better, Rosie. I can't live without you. I love you!" He kissed her forehead and remorsefully wept, heaving with pangs of repentance. She ached to wrap her arms around him, but they would not budge.

Chad quieted and then softly requested, "Rose, I need Jesus. Please lead me to Him!"

Rosie's body ignored her attempts, but her spirit fought for her the battle of desire. Slowly, her lips began pursing the words, "Repeat after me . . . Father."

Chad quietly repeated, "Father."

"Forgive me of my sins. Save me, Jesus. I need You!" Chad whispered his cry to God, and immediately his sins were forgiven. His eyes tightened for several minutes as he spoke to God, and Wisdom Angel Narcissus removed the label, PRODIGAL. Weights of one thousand unseen pounds were lifted from his shoulders, and he experienced a lightness and a freedom not known since his childhood.

After a few moments time, Chad again gazed upon Rosie's face. The sweet, serene peace on her face comforted Chad . . . until abruptly the head nurse rushed in with a host of other white-dressed soldiers clamoring about, pushing him to the side and administering all types of maneuvers that unnerved him and brought his soul confusion. His body began to tremble as the scenario of life-saving health measures were unveiled before his eyes.

Then, suddenly, there was silence. The haunting, quiet voice of the head nurse regretfully spoke, splitting the silence, "She's gone. We've lost her!"

Chad sprang from his stupor and cried, "That can't be. I was just talking to her. No! No! Rosie, come back, come back. You're just asleep. Don't leave me now. No, not now. I can't live without you. No, Rosie. No, don't leave me. Oh, God, dear God, bring her back. Bring her back!"

But it was too late . . . Rosie was already a universe away approaching her heart's desire, the very throne of the Living God.

## Chapter Fifteen
# Well Done

With only Angel Narcissus remaining with Chad, the widower was left alone at Rosie's bedside before making final arrangements with the nursing staff. Chad reached for Rosie's Bible sitting on the night stand that Andrew had wisely grabbed for his mother on their way out to the ambulance. Angel Narcissus gently blew open the pages to a hand-written poem by Rosie that read:

*The Words, "Well done, good and faithful servant," are like salve to my soul.*
*God alone has walked in my moccasins.*
*Only He knows the caliber of one's quiet solitude and gentle submission.*
*No one knows greater than He the pain of sacrifice.*
*I clutch His Word to my breast;*
*for to please Him is my greatest Joy!*
*The price is not too great to pay*
*for the hour I shall stand before Him*
*face to face and hear,*
***"Well done, good and faithful servant;***
***You have been faithful over a few things,***
***I will make you ruler over many things.***
***Enter into the joy of your Lord."***
                    ***Matthew 25:23.***

Chad now understood where Rosie was and why she had always positively responded to any mention of death—that to her it was life's reward. He placed her limp fingers in his palm and quietly whispered, "I love you . . . you're home now . . . and I understand . . . I'm sorry I made life so rough for you, and I know you forgive me . . . I'll do my best to walk with God and guide our children in His ways . . . I need you right now, more than ever . . . I just want to say what I should have said thousands of times before . . . well done . . . you were good to me . . . I'll make it up to you . . . you just watch and see . . . enjoy your reward, babe . . . I'll miss you . . . I will love you forever!"

In humble repentance, Chad kissed his "sweet angel Rose" good-bye. Being escorted by Angel Narcissus and closely clutching to his breast Rosie's *teddy bear*, the Living Word of God, Chad's heavy feet somberly shuffled toward the direction of the door. Glancing back at his princess, he softly spoke, "I have your sword —our sword!" That sword would prove to become his own source of strength for the rest of his days without her.

*"Precious in the sight of the Lord is*
*the death of His saints." Psalm 116:15.*

## Chapter Sixteen
# The Red Velveteen Cloak

One week had passed since Chad said good-bye to his Angel Rose. The memorial service had been an inspiring tribute to Rosie's loyalty as a Christian mother and wife. Chad had heard the gospel spoken with listening ears of his heart, and he had understood the promise of Heaven. Pastor Newberry's words were seeds that embedded themselves deeply within his repentant soul. Abigail, Tabitha, and Andrew had clung close to their daddy's side since Rosie's burial. No words of comfort from his mouth seemed adequate. He draped his long arms around his little lambs continually expressing his undying love to them with intense and painful hugs and strong grasps about their shoulders. No words could console their bereaved and broken hearts. This was a haunting ache that Chad would have to outwardly buffer but inwardly petition God to heal.

It was Saturday morning, and for the first time since Rosie's death, Chad was alone in his house. Abigail and Tabitha were visiting Grandma Windelton, and Andrew had gone to a YMCA basketball game with his cousin Mike. Chad's eyes glanced from wall to wall, light fixture to carpet, cupboard to curtain. It didn't matter what his eyes landed upon, they all screamed, "Rosie!" He saw her in every cloth and particle of their home. He gazed upon the picture hanging on the living room wall. It was an old well with daisies in the background—a simple picture to the common eye, but for Chad, one glance upon the well led to a piercing domino effect within the chambers of his memory. He journeyed back into time to an old well in his parents' back yard upon which he had first, at age seventeen, tenderly whispered into Rosie's innocent ears, "I love you!"

There was no escaping the haunting and mental visions and piercing flashbacks that cut like chainsaws into the lining of his soul. He was bleeding internally in an intangible way that no doctor or drug could affect.

Driven with the madness of insanity's cry, his knees buckled beneath him, and he fell on the floor, a sobbing heap of flesh and bones. His pain roared and bellowed, and for the first time, his deepest anguish and despair was given voice.

Angel Narcissus gently collected his tears, jar after jar, as the Holy Spirit of God wrapped a red velveteen cloak of comfort about the widower's shoulders. The black shroud of death was mournfully placed at the feet of Jesus as Chad cried out, "God! Oh, my God! Help me!" Instantaneously, Angel Narcissus was joined with a regiment of assisting comrades who set about ministering to their saint of God.

As Chad released his broken heart to his Heavenly Father, an anointing from the red velveteen cloak began oozing out of its fibers. Chad experienced a fiery sensation in every cell of his body, and then, a perfect peace enveloped his soul and quieted his spirit. The faucet of tears was gently turned off, and he knew that he was not alone in the room. It seemed that Rosie was somehow present with him.

Chad froze in a holy stillness . . . he was in the presence of the Living God.  He could not speak, nor could he move any muscle of his body.  He only listened to the voice of the Spirit:

*Beloved, I love you, and I am sorry for your sorrow. As you continue to place your pain at my feet, I will come to you with my presence, and I will comfort you. This day, I cover you with my holy salve of peace, an ointment from Heaven that will ooze into your razored wounds and draw out the pain.*

*Beloved, Rosie is with Me and is about her Father's business!  It is not because of you that I have brought her home.  No, but you must trust my sovereignty in orchestrating the symphony of each man's life.*

*Beloved Chad, you are my son, and I love you. Jesus, my own Son, died for you and shed his blood on the cross to purchase your salvation and healing of soul.  He, too, died an early death.*

*Because you have humbled yourself today and called out my name, I have robed you with the velveteen presence of my Spirit, wrapped around your shoulders, ordained to comfort and soothe your aching heart.*

*Chad, I have given you three beautiful children, the fruit of your love for Rosie.  You are to raise them up in my Church and instruct them in my Word.  They will bring you comfort and joy.  I will heal their hearts, and I promise you a full and nurtured life in my Spirit with them.*

*Beloved, I love you.  Go now, and question no more. I will always be with you, even unto the day that you return to Me and embrace your dearly loved Rose.*

*Chad, I love you! I love you! I love you! It is just you and Me now. Cloaked in my Spirit of Comfort, together, we will face the wind—and you will make it! Amen.*

In a glistening moment's time, Chad began to hear what sounded like the far distant whisper of Rosie. Bolted to the floor and frozen in prostrate fashion, his ears burned with a song of Heaven:

**"And God will wipe away every tear**
 **from their eyes;**
**there shall be no more death,**
**nor sorrow,**
**nor crying.**
**There shall be no more pain,**
**for the former things have passed away.**
**He who overcomes shall inherit all things,**
**and I will be his God and he shall be My Son."**
**Revelation 21:4, 7.**
*Amen and amen.*

# Postlogue

The death of a young person can raise haunting and unsettling questions. This mystery of death is addressed on the following page.

*Earth's Good-bye Is Heaven's Hello* is an entry from **The Father's Voice,** a daily devotional by Rose Marie Jones © 1999.

# Earth's Good-bye Is Heaven's Hello!

*"The righteous perish, and no one ponders it in his heart; devout men are taken away, and no one understands that the righteous are taken away to be spared from evil."*          *Isaiah 57:1, NIV*

You must trust Me in all situations, especially when death's jaws have clamped themselves about the life of a dear one whose breath was yet young and strong.

Beloved, I see your aching heart, the desperation of your grief. My Holy Spirit, my Comforter, is ever present with you to absorb your pain and console your wounded feelings.

My dear one, you know that your beloved one is with Me, absorbed in my glory, basking in my full presence. Earth's strings have been cut only to loose your loved one to Me where he is finding completeness, wholeness, purity, and fulfillment of my peace.

You ask why, and I answer—I am God. Your beloved is with Me. Would you not also enjoy an early arrival into my Kingdom's glory?

Beloved, my comfort is your knowledge of exactly where it is that your beloved has come. If you could see into heaven and see us together, you would understand, and your sorrow would cease.

Your beloved's visa home came earlier than you had planned. My sovereignty prevails, and all things are made good in my hand. There is no sting in eternal life. Your beloved is with Me in heaven. I would have you rejoice because your name, too, is written in the Book of Life, and no accident or illness can affect the guarantee of eternal life with Me.

The blood of my Son, your Savior Jesus Christ, has purchased your salvation and eternal life with Me. Earth's death is heaven's birth. *Earth's good-bye is heaven's hello!*

Rejoice in your beloved's arrival to my throne. No more evil. No more labor. He is with Me now, and you must go on but not alone. We are with you in Spirit! We are with you! We are with you!

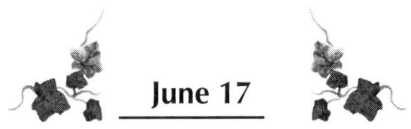

**June 17**

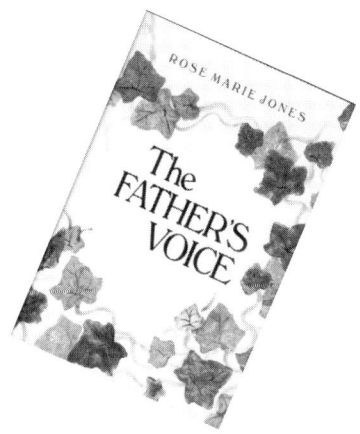

# The Father's Voice
## A Daily Devotional
by Rose Marie Jones

# ORDER FORM

NAME _____

STREET _____

CITY _____ STATE _____ ZIP _____

_____ @ $15.95 ........................................ $ _____
NUMBER OF
  BOOKS

SHIPPING: $2.00 PER BOOK ................. $ _____

SALES TAX: PLEASE ADD $1.00
PER BOOK FOR SHIPMENT TO
ILLINOIS ADDRESS .............................. $ _____

**TOTAL** ......................................... $ _____

**PLEASE RETURN ORDER FORM AND CHECK PAYABLE
TO:**

**VOICE PUBLISHING**

54 ALBION
JACKSONVILLE, ILLINOIS 62650

email: voicepublishing@myhtn.net

The Story of
Unfailing Love

# ORDER FORM

NAME _____

STREET _____

CITY _____ STATE _____ ZIP _____

_____ @ $8.00 ......................................... $ _____
NUMBER OF
   BOOKS

             SHIPPING: $1.50 PER BOOK ................. $ _____

             SALES TAX: PLEASE ADD $.50
             PER BOOK FOR SHIPMENT TO
             ILLINOIS ADDRESS .............................. $ _____

                  TOTAL ......................................... $ _____

## PLEASE RETURN ORDER FORM AND CHECK PAYABLE
## TO:
## VOICE PUBLISHING

54 ALBION
JACKSONVILLE, ILLINOIS 62650

email: voicepublishing@myhtn.net